The Icing on the Cake

shalini latour

08 07 06 05 04   5 4 3 2 1

Library of Congress Cataloging-in-Publication Data

Latour, Shalini
    The icing on the cake / by Shalini Latour.
       p. cm.
    Includes index.
    ISBN 1-58180-493-8
    1. Cake decorating. I. Title.

    TX771.2.L38 2004
    641.8'6539--dc22
                        2004041539

Editor: Krista Hamilton
Designers: Joanna Detz, Karla Baker
Layout Artist: Amy Wilkin
Production Coordinator: Sara Dumford
Photographers: Christine Polomsky, Tim Grondin

About the Author

Originally from Montreal, Canada, Shalini currently
lives in Cincinnati, Ohio, with her dog, Andy. When
she is not making cakes for weddings, birthdays
and other special occasions, Shalini teaches yoga
at several studios in Cincinnati.

Shalini first began decorating cakes
while living in a meditation center in upstate New
York. As part of the staff, she worked in the bakery
and learned all about pastry bags, fondant, sugar
flowers and the art of edible decorations. She man-
aged the bakery there for several years and trained
the new recruits. During Shalini's years as a pastry
chef, she also attended cake decorating classes in
New York City with Scott Clark Woolley, a culinary
connoisseur whose cakes have graced the pages
of *Bride's* magazine and *Martha Stewart's
Weddings*. Shalini enjoys making and decorating
cakes almost as much as she enjoys eating them.

Dedication

This book is dedicated to my mom. She taught me how to bake, showed me how to appreciate delicious foods and always encouraged me to do what makes me happy.

Acknowledgments

I would like to thank Swami Chidvilasanda, who gave me the skills necessary to complete this project. In her care, I learned cake decorating and gained the confidence and knowledge needed to accomplish any task.

Dave Forrest needs to be acknowledged for his support, for helping me move and carry stuff around, for tactfully giving me feedback on cake design and for listening to all my whining, doubting and complaining through this whole process.

I am grateful to all my friends: Lynette, Laura, Susan, Julie, Jamie, Nikki, Rosana, Emily and Randy for their support in my moments of crisis and for letting me experiment on their wedding and birthday cakes!

Thanks to Wendy for generously offering advice.

My thanks to Krista Hamilton and Christine Polomsky. Working with them was great.

My dog Andy also deserves my gratitude for keeping the floors clear of any crumbs. My apologies for all the times we didn't go to the park so I could work on this book.

table of
contents

introduction

As a kid, my mom always let me "help" her in the kitchen. From the time I could hold a spoon, she taught me to cook and bake. Although she was (and still is) a great pastry chef, there came a time for her to pass down the apron. From the age of 10, I took over all baking in the house. My mom always taught me not to be afraid of the kitchen or anything in it, and to have fun. As I received more formal training and tried my hand at decorating and designing more elaborate cakes, the fun and satisfaction only grew.

One of my favorite things about decorating cakes is that they are edible – cakes are not permanent. There is no need to be overwhelmed by perfection since your masterpiece will soon be out of sight! Another fabulous thing about cake decorating is that everything is fixable. A broken cake can be mended with icing, unsatisfactory decorations can be scraped off and redone and a sprinkling of powdered sugar will disguise many a blemish.

All the projects in this book can be made in a normal size kitchen with basic tools. I live in a one-bedroom apartment with a small galley kitchen, and while some of my supplies spill into the dining area, space is never a problem. The kitchen table is always a great extension to counter space.

Some of the projects in this book are simple and quick, while others are a bit more challenging. All the techniques can be mastered with a little practice and patience. Don't be afraid to experiment and play. Surely your family and friends will be able to help make any of your mistakes disappear! Also, don't be afraid to make a mess. Flour on your face and icing in you hair are part of the experience!

I am delighted to be able to share with you everything you need to make cake decorating a fun, rewarding and tasty experience. I hope you will use the projects and techniques in this book as a stepping-stone for your own creations, and that you will have as much fun doing so as I did while working on this book. Bon appétit!

tools
and supplies

The tools and supplies shown in this book are common, everyday items that can be found in most cooking and craft stores. Dig around in your kitchen and you may find that you already have most of them!

Baking pans

Aluminum pans with straight edges work best when baking cakes. If the bottom surface is completely flat, an inexpensive pan works just as well as an expensive one. Keep in mind that darker pans absorb more heat and will brown your cake more quickly than a lighter, shiny pan. For most of the cakes in this book, I used an 8" (20cm) round baking pan.

Bowls

You will need plenty of bowls for mixing your cake batter and icing. I prefer to use stainless steel bowls because they take abuse well, but any ceramic or plastic bowl set will do.

Cardboard

Placing your cake on a piece of cardboard will allow you to move and store it more easily. Old pizza boxes cut and covered in aluminum foil are great for this! The cake should remain on the cardboard even as it is served. This will make it easier to store leftovers.

Cookie cutters

These are available in almost every shape and size. They can be found in craft and cookware stores, as well as in the baking aisle of many grocery stores. I use metal cookie cutters because they are more durable and have sharper edges. Aluminum cookie cutters also work well but can be bent easily. Plastic cookie cutters are very inexpensive and are available in most standard shapes, but they crack easily when firm pressure is applied.

Cookie sheets

You can never have too many of these, as they are perfect for holding finished cakes and royal icing decorations as they harden. They can also be used to bake sheet cakes (see Bugs and Bees on page 86). They come in various sizes, but the size I prefer is 9" x 13" (23cm x 33cm). The inexpensive aluminum pans found in the grocery store work great.

Craft knife

This tool will help when cutting out fondant shapes with precision. Make sure the blade is extremely sharp.

Cutting board

This will protect your countertop from cuts, scratches and stains. I have one board that I use strictly for cakes so they don't end up tasting like last night's dinner. I recommend using a plastic board, which is less likely to absorb taste and odor than a wooden board.

Floral ribbon

Floral ribbon is ideal for cake decorating because it does not absorb moisture or stains as easily as satin ribbon. It comes in a rainbow of colors and can be found in local craft stores.

Floral tape

I use green floral tape to wrap the stems of several flower decorations together in a cluster. For easier handling, cut the standard tape width in half.

Floral wire

Floral wire makes great stems for royal icing flowers such as Lily of the Valley (see page 58). You can pipe the icing right onto the wire. Green wire tends to look more natural. I prefer light green, but dark green is also available.

Flower nail

This tool is used to make royal icing flowers (see page 52). The icing is piped onto a piece of parchment paper secured to the flat surface of the tool with icing. The "nail" is then rotated to form the petals and leaves. It can be found in craft and cookware stores.

Foil, plastic wrap and containers

These supplies, which you may already have in your pantry, are essential for storing cakes, icing, decorations and supplies.

Loaf pans

Loaf pans are often used to make denser cakes such as pound cake. I used a 4" x 8" (10cm x 20cm) loaf pan to make the Chocolate Fall Cake (page 92).

Measuring cups and spoons

These tools, which come in metal or plastic, are used for measuring ingredients precisely. To guarantee a perfect cake, it is important to follow the recipe measurements to a tee.

Mixer

Stand mixers come with a flat paddle attachment, a hook and a whisk. The flat paddle is best for mixing cake batter and icing. The whisk is for whipping cream and egg whites, and for mixing royal icing. The hook is only used for making bread. All recipes and projects can be accomplished with a hand mixer and a bit of elbow grease, but if you are serious about cake decorating, treat yourself to a good stand mixer!

Oven thermometer

Since temperatures vary from one oven to another, I recommend using this gadget for guaranteed accuracy. Hang it from the rack in the center of your oven and preheat it to the appropriate temperature. When the oven is heated, check the temperature on the thermometer. Check the temperature again five minutes into the baking process.

Paintbrushes

For painting food coloring on fondant (see page 115, step 5), a small set of paintbrushes comes in very handy. I recommend purchasing a thin, round brush and a square, flat brush that you will use exclusively for cake decorating.

Parchment paper

This is essential for lining pans, as it will prevent your cakes from sticking to the bottom. It is also used to make pastry bags (see pages 23 and 24) and royal icing flowers on a flower nail (see page 52). In a pinch, wax paper may be used.

Pastry bags, tips and couplers

These tools are essential for piping beautiful cake decorations. A variety of tips are available individually or in sets and are categorized by the type of piping they produce (descriptions on right). You will learn more about pastry bags on page 22.

which tip
SHOULD I USE?

Round tips: These are the most frequently used tips for cake decorating. They are used for piping dots, stems, vines, cornelli and for writing. They range in size from #1 (very thin) to #10 (very thick). Most commonly, decorators use #2 or #4 when piping fine details. I use tip #7 to pipe the vertical lines in a basket weave design (see page 48, step 1).

Star tips: These versatile tips are used to pipe stars, curvy and zigzagged lines, shell borders and rosettes. They range in size from #13 (small) to #32 (extra large). The tip that is used most by decorators seems to be #16, but larger tips work better for larger cakes.

Rose tips: The teardrop shaped openings on these tips are great for making petals for flowers such as roses, pansies and geraniums. They can also be used to pipe ribbons and bows. The most commonly used tips are #101, #102, #103 and #104.

Leaf tips: These tips are used for piping leaves. The V-shaped opening gives the appearance of veins. Common leaf tips include #65 and #67. I use tip #67 to pipe the horizontal lines in a basket weave design (see page 48, step 2).

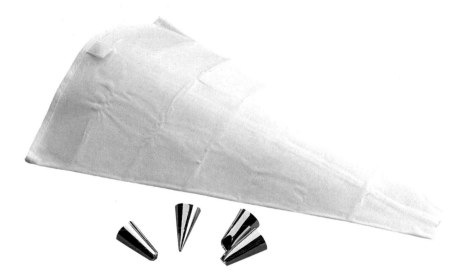

Pastry brush

A pastry brush dedicated to baking and decorating is essential for brushing cakes with sugar syrup. It also works well for painting larger areas of fondant with food coloring (see page 118, step 2).

Rolling pin

Your rolling pin should have a nice, smooth surface. I suggest using a plastic rolling pin, as some wooden rolling pins leave wood grain imprints in unwanted places.

Ruler

Cakes like White Chocolate Berry Fantasy require the precise measurements of a ruler (see page 82, step 2). I prefer to use a metal ruler, as it is very easy to clean.

Scraper, metal

Use this straight edge tool to smooth the sides and top of buttercream cakes like The Dots (see page 40, step 2).

Serrated knife

The sawlike edges of a serrated knife allow for easy cake slicing and leveling. To ensure clean cuts, wipe the blade with a towel dipped in warm water between cuts.

Sifter, large

A large, metal sifter is used for sifting flour, powdered sugar and other dry ingredients to remove lumps.

Sifter, small

The mini version of the large sifter is perfect for sprinkling powdered sugar, cocoa and cinnamon onto cakes.

Spatula, metal

Bent metal spatulas in large and small sizes are ideal for spreading and smoothing icing onto cakes. They can also be used to transfer cakes onto serving platters.

Spatula, rubber

This is used to scrape the cake batter and icing from the bowl so nothing goes to waste!

Straight edge knife

A large, sharp, straight edge kitchen knife is great for cutting, scoring and making chocolate curls and shavings, as shown in Springtime Garden (see page 55, step 14).

Turntable

This is one of the most wonderful cake decorating secrets. You can purchase a turntable at any craft store or use an old lazy Susan. The tool allows you to decorate your cake on a revolving base rather than rotating the cake itself.

Wire rack

This is for cooling cakes and pouring on icing without dripping it onto a serving plate. In a pinch, use an oven rack or a toaster oven rack.

Wire whisk

This tool is wonderful for whipping up meringue, egg whites and whipped cream.

in the
pantry

When it comes to baking, nothing is more important than a well-stocked pantry. I recommend keeping these easy-to-find ingredients on hand at all times.

Dairy

Cream is an essential ingredient in many filling and icing recipes. Heavy cream, also known as whipping cream, holds its shape well and can be used to fill a cake or to pipe decorations.

Many kinds of milk are used in baking. I use whole milk, which contains a high fat content and adds a rich, creamy taste to cakes. Low-fat and nonfat milks can also be used as a healthy substitute. If substituting, remember that the change in fat and water content may alter the taste and consistency of your cake.

Buttermilk is thick and creamy, with a mildly acidic taste. It is made from skim milk and milk powder and is cultured much like yogurt.

Most dairy products can be found in the powdered form, but I don't recommend using it unless the recipe specifically calls for it. It will alter the taste and consistency.

Eggs

Eggs are an important ingredient in baked goods, as they add structure, moisture, leavening qualities, flavor and nutritional value. I always use large or extra large eggs when baking. In most cases, you should take them out of the refrigerator an hour or two ahead of time. Cold eggs added to butter will make the butter harden and the mixture will appear to curdle. Mix it for a while on a medium to high speed until it regains a smooth texture. To quickly bring eggs to room temperature, submerge them in a bowl of warm water for 20 minutes.

While room-temperature eggs are best for batters, it is easier to separate eggs when they are cold. To separate an egg, carefully crack it on the side of a bowl. Hold the egg over the bowl and tip it back and forth between the two shells until the white has dripped into the bowl and the yolk remains in the shell. Be sure not to let any yolk in with the white or it will not whip properly. Also, keep egg whites away from water, as it will also impede whipping.

In recipes like icing, where the eggs are not cooked, I recommend using pasteurized eggs since they do not contain salmonella. I use pasteurized egg whites in most icing. They are readily available in grocery stores, easy to use and give icing a soft, fluffy texture.

Some people also prefer dried, or powdered, egg whites, which can be reconstituted by adding water. These work well for royal icing. Your local craft store should carry these in the cake decorating aisle.

Extracts and imitation flavorings

Extracts are made from essential oils extracted from the original food from which they take their flavor. Popular extracts include almond, orange, peppermint and vanilla.

Unlike extracts, imitation flavorings do not contain any elements of the original food. This makes the flavor less potent. Some common imitation flavorings include vanilla, cherry, coconut, pineapple, brandy and rum.

Fats and oils

Butter is my first choice for baking, as it gives cake and icing the perfect taste, texture and consistency. Make sure the butter is softened, either by removing it from the refrigerator an hour before baking or by microwaving it for a few

seconds. (Not too long. You don't want to melt it!)

Margarine can also be used in cakes but cannot be substituted for butter. Their different contents of water and fat produce very different results. If you must use margarine, seek out a recipe specifically tested with it.

Vegetable shortening is a solid fat made from vegetable oils. It is used in fondant and many flaky baked goods such as pie crust. It can be stored at room temperature for up to a year.

Many recipes call for cooking oil, which should not be substituted for solid fat. Common oils used for baking include canola oil, sunflower oil and vegetable oil, which have a mild taste. Olive oil is not used in dessert recipes because of its rich flavor.

Flour

There are so many different types of flour used for baking. Making a choice can be very overwhelming. While all types of flour serve their purpose for different confections, I find that all-purpose white flour works best for my cakes.

Many bakers prefer the delicate texture of cake flour for lighter cakes like angel food. Others prefer the nuttier taste of wheat flour. Self-rising flour, bread flour, rye four and soy flour may also be used. Be sure to use the type of flour specified in your recipe. If it simply says "flour," all-purpose white flour is usually assumed.

Fruit

Fresh fruit is a healthy, colorful and tasty addition to any recipe. It is wonderful for filling and decorating cakes.

The peel of citrus fruit, called zest, adds a tangy zing to white and yellow cakes. Strawberries, raspberries, blueberries, blackberries and cherries are also great for filling and decorating cakes.

Although frozen fruit cannot be used as a decoration, it can be substituted for fresh fruit as a filling. It is especially useful in the winter, when many fresh fruits are out of season.

Leavening agents

Common leavening agents used in baking include yeast (used mostly for baking bread), baking powder and baking soda. They contain chemicals that produce carbon dioxide, which allows baked goods to rise during preparation and baking. One should not be substituted for another, as they each have specific uses in baking.

Recipes that call for baking soda contain some acidic ingredients, such as lemon juice, sour cream or buttermilk. When the baking soda reacts with the acid, it immediately produces carbon dioxide bubbles that allow the batter to rise. Therefore the cake should be baked immediately after adding this ingredient, before the bubbles pop.

Baking powder already contains baking soda and an acidic ingredient, such as cream of tartar, that activates the production of carbon dioxide. Single acting baking powder, which is not widely available, is activated when liquid is added. Double acting baking powder, which is most common for baking, is activated first when liquid is added, and then again when heat is added. This is why recipes using baking powder require dry ingredients to be combined first.

Spices

Spices add richness to ordinary recipes. Common spices include cinnamon, nutmeg, cloves, allspice and ginger. It is important to note that spices can have a drying effect on baked goods. To avoid this, decrease the amount of flour in proportion to the amount of spices used.

Sweeteners

Sweeteners are essential for adding flavor and texture to baked goods. Granulated sugar, or white sugar, is most commonly used in baking.

Brown sugar is a mixture of granulated sugar and molasses. It is available in dark and light varieties and adds a hint of caramel flavor.

Powdered sugar, also called confectioner's sugar, is granulated sugar that is ground into a fine powder, then mixed with cornstarch to keep it from getting lumpy. It is a primary ingredient in most icing and filling recipes, and it can also be sprinkled over finished cakes as a decoration.

Molasses is a thick, dark brown syrup made from sugarcane. It is most commonly used to sweeten ginger snaps and gingerbread. Corn syrup is a heavy syrup with half the sweetness of sugar. It is available in light and dark varieties and is similar in taste to brown sugar. Honey, made by bees from flower nectar, adds an extremely sweet and distinct flavor to baked goods.

warming up

Before you begin baking and decorating, there are a few things to keep in mind. First, don't be intimidated by any of the projects. Icing can always be taken off the cake and redone. I keep an extra tub of icing in the fridge for those eventualities myself.

Be sure to read the entire instructions of a project before you start. Some of the decorations, such as royal icing flowers, must be made ahead of time to allow for hardening or setting. It is best to budget your time so that you can finish everything by the time your cake is needed.

Gather all the supplies and ingredients before you start. You wouldn't want to stop in the middle of decorating to run to the store. Most ingredients are available in your local grocery store, and you should be able to find all the supplies at your local craft store. If you have a cake decorating specialty store in your area, be sure to pay them a visit for ideas.

Finally, move everything you don't need out of the way to give yourself plenty of working space. Most of the decorating process happens while standing up, but it is good to have a chair or stool handy to sit down when you can. Otherwise, you will end up with sore feet.

Now you're ready to put on your apron, plug in your mixer, turn on the oven and start creating!

Temperature and Oven Basics

The temperature of the room you are working in can affect your baking results. A cool room with low humidity works best.

It is also very important to get to know your oven. Each oven has its own temperament, and we must adapt accordingly. Even a brand new convection oven will take some getting used to. Some ovens tend to be hotter or cooler than the temperature selected. Some bake unevenly from top to bottom or side to side. There are a couple of easy solutions to these problems:

• Purchase an oven thermometer to test the precise temperature while baking. Hang it from your oven rack and check it often.

• Move your oven rack up or down to adjust for cakes that are baking unevenly from top to bottom.

• Place cakes off-center to compensate for cakes that are baking unevenly from side to side.

tasty TIDBIT In hot, humid conditions, make your icing a bit stiffer by adding powdered sugar to buttercream or fondant.

How to Tell if a Cake is Done

It bears repeating that baking times always vary. The weather, the humidity, your oven and your ingredients will affect how long a cake should stay in the oven. There are two methods I use to determine whether a cake is done.

1. Toothpick Method

Remove the cake from the oven and insert a toothpick into the center of the cake. The toothpick should come out dry. If it comes out wet, bake the cake for a few more minutes and test it again.

2. Finger Method

Remove the cake from the oven and press down on the center of the cake with your finger. The cake will spring back when it is done.

How to Line a Pan

Lining your baking pan with parchment paper will allow you to easily remove the cake from the pan once it is done.

tasty TIDBIT For accurate measuring, use a pencil to trace around the bottom of the baking pan onto the parchment paper.

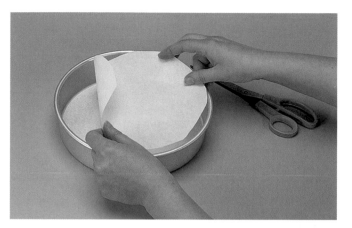

Line Pan with Paper

Brush a small amount of cooking oil or butter onto the bottom and sides of your baking pan with a pastry brush or your fingers. Next, cut parchment paper to the size of the bottom of the pan and place it inside the pan.

How to Remove a Cake from a Pan

Removing a cake from a properly lined pan is as easy as 1-2-3!

1. Run Knife Along Pan

When the cake is cool to the touch, hold a straight edge knife in one hand and place the other hand on the cake. Run the knife along the edge of the pan.

2. Flip Pan

Flip the pan over onto a piece of cardboard and lift the pan. Tap on the pan with the knife handle to help loosen the cake.

3. Remove Paper

Peel the parchment paper from the bottom of the cake.

How to Level a Cake

Cakes often bake with peaks on the top or uneven sides. Leveling your cake will make it nice and flat.

 **tasty TIDBIT** I like using the bottom of the cake as my top layer since it is already flat.

Cut Cake Top

Place the baked cake on a piece of cardboard. Using one hand to stabilize the cake, insert a serrated knife into the side of the cake near the top. Work the knife around the cake, rotating slowly. Remove the top layer and set it aside. Your cake top is now flat.

How to Fill a Cake

As you fill a cake, feel free to add your favorite fruit and flavoring between the layers, as this is the part that will make it not only beautiful but also delicious. Use more stable fillings like ganache and buttercream for elaborate cakes since they will be out of the refrigerator for long periods of time while you decorate them.

 **tasty TIDBIT** Always place your cake on a cake cardboard before adding syrup and filling so that it can be handled more easily.

1. Cut and Remove Top Layer

To cut a cake into layers, insert a serrated knife into the side of the cake about two-thirds of the way from the bottom and cut all the way around the cake. Remove the top layer and set it aside. Repeat this process to make middle and bottom layers. Transfer the bottom layer to a round piece of cardboard.

2. Spread Syrup

Using a pastry brush, spread a generous amount of sugar syrup (recipe on page 30) over the bottom layer. The sugar syrup will add moisture and sweetness to the cake.

3. Add Filling

Transfer the cake and cardboard to a turntable. Spoon the filling of your choice onto the bottom layer of the cake. You will need about 1 ½ cups (355ml) of filling per layer for an 8" (20cm) cake.

4. Spread Filling

Spread the filling evenly with a spatula, rotating the turntable for an even coating.

tasty
TIDBIT Sugar syrup adds moisture to cakes, but it also makes them wet and crumbly. To avoid unnecessary handling, brush the syrup onto each layer before you add the filling. Covering the entire cake with syrup before filling it may result in a broken cake.

5. Stack and Add More Filling

Place the middle layer on top of the bottom layer, brush with sugar syrup and add more filling. Spread the filling evenly with a spatula. Place the final layer on top and add another coating of sugar syrup.

6. Pack Tightly with Hands

Pack the sides and top of the cake with your hands to evenly distribute the filing.

How to Crumb-Coat a Cake

The purpose of a crumb coat is to seal in moisture and cake crumbs. Therefore, it is okay to see a little of the cake through the coating. This is because you will add another layer of icing that will cover it once the crumb coat has set. You will need about 1½ to 2 cups of icing to crumb-coat an 8" (20cm) cake.

tasty
TIDBIT Start by covering the sides of the cake, then work your way to the top so that the cake doesn't crumble under the weight of the icing.

1. Add Icing

Spoon a mound of buttercream icing (recipe on page 30) onto the top of the cake.

2. Spread Over Sides

Use a spatula to spread the icing over the sides of the cake, working back and forth with your wrist.

3. Spread Over Top

Spread the remaining icing over the top of the cake.

4. Refrigerate Until Set

Use your spatula to remove the excess icing from the cake. Refrigerate for a minimum of two hours. For best results, refrigerate overnight. Reserve the rest of the icing for a final coat or for decorations.

Color Basics

The perfect icing color plays an important role in your cake's overall appearance. Bright, vibrant reds, blues and greens may be perfect for a birthday cake but inappropriate for a traditional wedding cake. On the other hand, not enough color may make a cake look bland. Finding the right balance is essential!

Here are a few tips that will help you achieve the right colors when working with food coloring:

- Add a bit of yellow to brighten up a dull green.

- Add a bit of red for a more natural green used to make leaves.

How to Color Icing

I recommend using food coloring paste, rather than liquid food coloring, to keep the consistency of the icing intact. Add color a little at a time. It is easy to add more color, but impossible to take it away. Also, make sure you color enough icing for your whole project. Matching icing color is challenging and you want to avoid it if possible.

- To achieve a vibrant red instead of a pinkish red, add a generous amount of food coloring paste.

- Black, like red, requires an ample amount of food coloring paste to get the true, rich color.

- Pink comes out better with food coloring paste that is pink, burgundy or rose rather than red.

- Add a little brown or orange to soften a bright yellow.

- The longer icing sits, the darker it becomes. If you are making your colors ahead of time, make them lighter than your desired color.

- If you must use liquid food coloring and your icing becomes too runny, add a bit of powdered sugar to thicken it.

1. Add Icing to Bowl

Spoon the desired amount of icing into a bowl.

tasty
TIDBIT The only food coloring that is not available in paste form is white, therefore liquid food coloring must be used.

2. Add Color to Toothpick

Dip a toothpick into the jar of food coloring paste.

3. Tint Icing with Toothpick

Dip the toothpick into the icing and swirl it around to distribute the color evenly. Mix with a rubber spatula.

Pastry Bag Basics

Pastry bags are one of the most important tools in cake decorating. They allow us to pipe icing in different shapes and sizes to make our decorations. Bags are made of cloth and come in a variety of sizes from very small (6" [15cm]) to very large (20" [51cm]). I prefer a medium-sized (14" [36cm]) bag for piping buttercream and something a bit smaller (10" - 12" [25cm - 30cm]) for piping royal icing.

Each pastry bag requires a coupler, which is a plastic piece that fits on the end of the bag. The coupler allows you to change the decorating tip without transferring the icing to another bag. It comes in two parts: the base and the ring. The base fits inside the bag, and the ring fits over the decorating tip to hold it in place.

Tips are open-ended metal pieces that come in different shapes and sizes. Star tips are used for borders; round tips are used for writing and for making vines and dots; leaf tips are great for just what their name suggests; and rose tips make roses and other flowers. Tips are available in sets, which will give you a nice variety of decorating options. (For more information about the different kinds of tips, see page 10.) Be sure to experiment with them all and find out what they can do!

How to Fill a Pastry Bag

The trick to filling a pastry bag is to keep the icing away from the wide end of the bag. Otherwise, it may squeeze back out and make a mess. Always keep the wide end twisted tightly when piping to avoid this backflow.

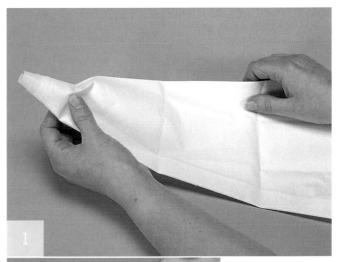

1. Insert Coupler

Cut off the tip of a pastry bag and insert the base of the coupler into the tapered end.

2. Spoon in Icing

Fold the wide end of the bag inside out. Place one hand under the folded part of the bag, gripping the tapered end, and use the other hand to spoon icing into the bag.

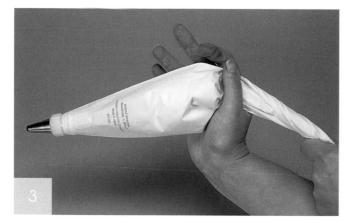

tasty
TIDBIT Practice writing and making your decorations on a
cutting board or hard surface to get
used to the consistency of the icing.
Practice makes perfect!

3. Add Tip

Position the desired pastry tip on the pointed end of
the bag and screw on the coupler ring. Twist the
wide end of the bag, pushing the icing toward the tip.

How to Make Your Own Pastry Bag

Pastry bags made of parchment paper are easy
to make and useful for chocolate and runny icing,
which are hard to clean from cloth bags. They are
also used for decorations that do not require tips,
like simple lines or writing (see page 78, step 3).

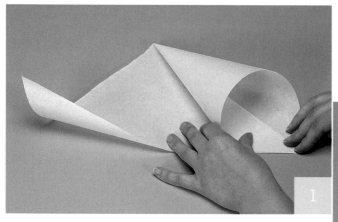

1. Prepare Parchment Paper

Cut a piece of parchment paper into a triangle
and roll the edges so the far corners fold in like
a cone. Make sure the point is nice and tight,
with no opening.

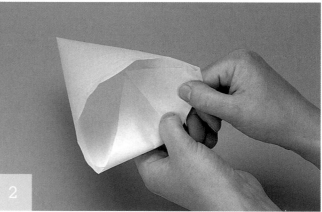

2. Tuck Ends

Tuck the wide ends inside the cone to hold the
shape in place.

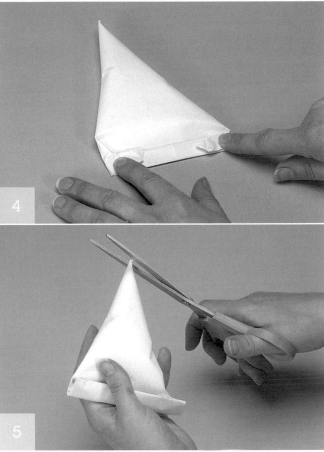

3. Fill with Icing

Fill the pastry bag with icing and crease the wide end of the bag a couple of times to seal in the contents.

4. Fold Edges

Fold in the outside edges of the bag to further secure it.

5. Cut Tip

Cut off the very tip of the bag, about ⅛" (0.3cm) or the desired opening size. Be careful not to make the opening too large or the icing will pour out all at once.

How to Store Cakes and Ingredients

Wrapped tightly in cellophane and refrigerated, an undecorated cake will keep for two to three days without affecting the taste. If you need to make a cake further ahead of time, it will keep in the freezer for up to one month. I recommend wrapping it in two layers of cellophane to keep it from drying out. Thaw the cake by transferring it from the freezer to the refrigerator a few hours before you need it.

Icing keeps best in an airtight container in the refrigerator and can also be made ahead of time to lighten your load on decoration day. Buttercream icing must be taken out of the refrigerator several hours before you use it, and it must be whipped with a mixer to regain its smooth consistency. Ganache must be melted before use. Fondant must be warmed up a bit so that it is soft enough to handle.

Finished cakes can simply be refrigerated until they are served; the outer layer of icing will seal in the moisture. Be sure to cover leftover cake with wax paper or cellophane directly in contact with the open portion of the cake to preserve it and keep it moist.

How to Present Your Masterpiece

The way you present your masterpiece can greatly enhance its appearance. Choose a plate that accents and complements your cake but does not steal the show. Large cake platters work best, as they usually do not have rims. A lower area in the middle of a platter tends to make a cake look smaller. Plain glass platters and large gold platters work for almost any cake. I often try out a few different platters before settling on the one I like best.

For special occasions, you may choose to accent your presentation with doilies, colored napkins and fancy tablecloths. Another way to showcase a beautiful cake is to place it on a cake stand. To make your own cake stand, place a cardboard box under your tablecloth and arrange the cake on top. Then place napkins, plates and silverware on the lower section of the table.

troubleshooting tips

PROBLEM	POSSIBLE CAUSE
Cake didn't rise.	Too much water or oil.
	Pan too large.
	Oven temperature too low and/or cake underbaked.
	Ingredients underbeaten.
	Batter sat too long before baking.
Cake shrunk.	Too much water or oil.
	Oven temperature too high and/or cake overbaked.
	Ingredients overbeaten.
Cake is soggy/dense/heavy.	Cake underbaked and/or removed before done baking.
	Oven door opened during baking.
	Too much water or oil.
	Ingredients under- or overbeaten.
Cake is dry/crumbly.	Oven temperature too high and/or cake overbaked.
	Not enough water, oil or egg.
Cake is split down middle.	Ingredients overbeaten.
Cake ran over sides of pan.	Oven temperature too low.
	Too much batter in pan (fill no more than ⅔ full).
	Too much water.
	Pan or oven rack not level.
	Pan placed off-center in oven.
Cake is sticking to pan.	Pan not greased or lined with parchment paper.
	Cake not cooled long enough.
	Cake not loosened with knife or spatula before removing.
Cake is difficult to frost.	Cake not completely cool.
	Frosting not proper consistency.

basic
recipes

An undecorated cake is like a blank canvas in the world of edible art. Even the most elaborate cakes start with a few basic ingredients and simple steps. The cake recipes in this section are just a few of the many that I recommend.

If you're in a time crunch, store-bought cake mixes are also an option. While homemade cakes are usually tastier, adding a bit of flavoring to a store-bought mix will greatly improve its taste and allow you to create new flavor combinations of your own. I recommend adding the zest of a lemon or orange (or both!) to white or yellow cake for a fresh, tangy taste. You can also add instant coffee powder to chocolate cakes for a richer flavor. Brandy and rum improve the taste of pretty much anything. In addition, liquor tends to cut the

sweetness. However you decide to doctor up your cake mix, be creative and have fun!

Always line your pan, preheat your oven and lick the bowl before you wash it! As you blend the ingredients, be careful not to overmix the batter, as it will give your cake a tough consistency. I recommend baking your cake 24 hours ahead of time and storing it in the refrigerator until you are ready to decorate it. This will allow it to set, making it easier to work with and less crumbly.

In addition to cake recipes, I have also included recipes for filling and icing. They, too, can be adjusted to your liking. Just remember, the filling must be stiff enough to stabilize the cake so the layers will not top-

ple over, and the icing must be the right consistency depending on whether you use it for crumb-coating, covering or decorating your cake. The amount of icing used will vary depending on whether you cover your cake in a thick or thin layer.

Each project begins with a basic iced or uniced cake, which is listed under "Ingredients You'll Need." Other ingredients listed include specific quantities of icing used for decorating. Although each icing recipe in this section makes one quantity, a full quantity of icing may not be required. Therefore, it may be necessary to scale down the recipe as appropriate. Many of the icings must also be colored prior to decorating. This process is described on page 21.

cakes

The following recipes are for one thick 8" (20cm) round cake (3" [7.6cm] tall baking pan) or a thinner 9" (23cm) round cake. Either cake will serve 12 people easily. To make a square 8" (20cm) cake or a thicker 9" (23cm) round cake, increase the recipe ingredients by 25% and the baking time by 5 to 15 minutes. To make a 9" x 13" (23cm x 33cm) sheet cake, use the standard recipe and pour the batter into a cookie sheet lined with parchment paper. Fill the cookie sheet almost to the top. The baking time will be shorter since the cake is thin.

Chocolate Cake

This light cake with rich, chocolaty flavor is easy to make and handle because it does not crumble.

1c + 2 tbsp (250g/9oz) butter, softened
1½ c (300g/11oz) sugar
1 tsp (5ml) vanilla extract
3 eggs
2¼ c (257g/9oz) all-purpose flour
¾ tsp (3.75ml) baking soda
¼ (1ml) tsp salt
½ c (41g/1.5oz) cocoa powder
2 tsp (10ml) instant coffee powder
1c + 2 tbsp (255ml/9fl oz) whole milk

1. Preheat oven to 350°F/180°C/Gas 4.
2. In a large bowl, beat butter and sugar with an electric mixer until mixture is light in color and fluffy in consistency.
3. Add vanilla.
4. Add eggs one at a time, beating well.
5. In a separate bowl, sift dry ingredients together.
6. Add half of the dry ingredients to the butter mixture, then half of the milk, then more dry ingredients and more milk. Continue until all ingredients are added. Do not overmix. (You may start on the next addition before the previous one is completely mixed in.)
7. Pour batter into a pan lined with parchment paper and bake 40 to 50 minutes.

White Cake

Substituting egg whites for whole eggs in this recipe make this cake light on fat but not on taste! This goes well with any filling flavor.

2⅓ c (270g/9½oz) all-purpose flour
1 tbsp (15ml) baking powder
¾ tsp (4ml) salt
1½ c (300g/11oz) sugar
½ c (75g/3oz) vegetable shortening
3 egg whites
1 c (250ml/8fl oz) whole milk
1 tsp (5ml) vanilla extract

1. Preheat oven to 350°F/180°C/Gas 4.
2. In a large bowl, sift together flour, baking powder, salt and sugar.
3. Cut in shortening until fine crumbs are formed.
4. In a separate bowl, whip egg whites until they form stiff peaks.
5. Add egg whites, milk and vanilla to crumb mixture.
6. Beat on low speed for one minute, then on high speed for two minutes, scraping the bowl frequently.
7. Pour batter into a pan lined with parchment paper and bake for 25 to 30 minutes.

Golden Butter Cake

This delicious, buttery cake is lighter than pound cake but with all the flavor. Add lemon zest to vary the taste.

1 c (300g/8oz) butter
1⅓ c (270g/11oz) sugar
4 eggs
1 tbsp (15ml) vanilla extract
1 tbsp (15ml) baking powder
3 c (350g/12oz) all-purpose flour
¾ c (180ml/6fl oz) whole milk

1. Preheat oven to 350°F/180°C/Gas 4.
2. In a large bowl, beat butter and sugar together until light in color.
3. Add eggs one at a time, beating well.
4. Add vanilla.
5. Add baking powder and half the flour.
6. Add half the milk. Add the remaining flour and milk, and mix but do not overmix.
7. Pour batter into a pan lined with parchment paper and bake for 1 hour to 1 hour and 10 minutes.

Chocolate Buttercream Icing

This is a delicious alternative to classic buttercream icing. The cream cheese gives it a slightly tart taste and makes it rich and creamy. It can be used as icing or filling and will keep for up to two weeks in the refrigerator. This recipe makes more than enough to crumb-coat and cover an 8" (20cm) round cake.

1 c (250g/8oz) butter
1 c (250g/8oz) cream cheese
2 tbsp (30ml) pasteurized egg whites
6 c (685g) powdered sugar
1 tsp (5ml) vanilla extract
1 tbsp (15ml) instant coffee powder
½ c (4oz) unsweetened chocolate, melted

1. Beat butter and cream cheese together with an electric mixer.
2. Add egg whites.
3. Add powdered sugar, vanilla and coffee.
4. Add melted chocolate, mixing well for a smooth consistency.

Cream Cheese Icing

This icing goes best with carrot cake. It can also be used in place of buttercream icing to crumb-coat a cake. This recipe makes enough to crumb-coat one 8" (20cm) round cake.

1 c (225g/8 oz) cream cheese
½ c (115g/4 oz) butter
2 tsp (10ml) vanilla extract
2 c (230g/8oz) powdered sugar

1. Whip cream cheese and slowly add butter.
2. Add vanilla and powdered sugar.
3. Beat well.

Chocolate Ganache

Ganache is a rich combination of chocolate and cream that makes a smooth, shiny icing. It keeps well for up to two weeks when refrigerated and can be remelted in the microwave. Do not overheat, as ganache burns easily. This recipe makes more than enough to cover one 8" (20cm) round cake.

½ c + 2 tbsp (130ml/5fl oz) heavy cream
1 c (8oz) semisweet chocolate

1. Heat cream in sauce pan until boiling. Remove from heat.
2. Add chocolate and mix with wooden spoon until melted and mixture is smooth.
3. Allow to cool.

White Chocolate Ganache

This variation can also be whipped and used as a filling or icing. If you wish to add pizzazz to your ganache, substitute 1 tbsp (15ml) of a flavoring such as amaretto or orange liqueur for 1 tbsp (15ml) of cream. This recipe makes more than enough to cover one 8" (20cm) round cake.

⅓ c (90ml/3fl oz) heavy cream
1½ c (12oz) white chocolate chips

1. Bring cream to a boil. Remove from heat and add white chocolate chips.
2. Add flavoring if desired. Mix well.
3. Allow to cool.

tasty TIDBIT To whip ganache, warm it so that it is soft but not hot to the touch. Pour the warm ganache into an electric mixer bowl and whip it with the wire whisk attachment until it is light in color and fluffy in consistency. Do not over-whip or it may curdle.

Royal Icing

Make the royal icing just before you need it, as it does not last more than one or two days. Royal icing dries very quickly, and unused portions should be covered with cellophane in direct contact with the icing to avoid exposure to the air. If you have any leftover icing after making the decorations you need, I recommend making extra royal icing decorations for future use. Dried royal icing decorations last for months if they are stored in an airtight container. This recipe makes 2 cups (16oz).

2 pasteurized egg whites
3 c (342g) powdered sugar

1. Whip egg whites with an electric mixer.
2. As they start to frost and turn white, add powdered sugar.
3. Whip for 5 to 10 minutes, until stiff peaks form.

Fondant

Rolled fondant, also called sugar paste, is used to cover cakes with an extra smooth finish, giving them the appearance of porcelain. This recipe makes more than enough to cover an 8" (20cm) round cake, with enough left over for a small border.

1 tbsp (15ml) gelatin
4 tbsp (60ml) water
2 tbsp (25g/7oz) vegetable shortening
½ c (200g/7oz) white corn syrup
1 tsp (15ml) clear flavoring of choice
7 c (800g) powdered sugar

1. In a double boiler, melt the gelatin and water. Dissolve all the gelatin, but do not bring it to a boil.
2. Remove from heat and add shortening. Mix until melted.
3. Add corn syrup and flavoring. Mix until blended.

4. Pour powdered sugar into mixing bowl and add wet ingredients. It will be thick and stiff like molding dough.
5. Sprinkle powdered sugar on work surface and grease your hands with shortening. Place fondant onto work surface and knead until it has a smooth consistency.
6. Wrap well in two layers of cellophane and refrigerate until needed.

tasty

TIDBIT To cover an 8" (20cm) square cake such as the Christmas Package cake on page 112, double the fondant recipe. You will have enough left over to use for decorations such as ribbons and bows.

baking terms

US BAKING TERMS	EUROPEAN BAKING TERMS
All-purpose flour	Plain flour
Baking soda	Bicarbonate of soda
Cream, half and half or light	Cream, single
Cream, heavy or whipping	Cream, double
Corn starch	Cornflour
Extract	Essence
Self-rising flour	Self-raising flour
Brown sugar	Light muscovado sugar
Granulated/fine/white sugar	Caster sugar
Corn syrup	Golden syrup
Confectioner's/powdered sugar	Icing sugar
Vegetable shortening	White vegetable fat

measurement conversions

KNOWN	MULTIPLY BY	NEEDED
Teaspoons (tsp)	4.93	Milliliters (ml)
Tablespoons (tbsp)	14.79	Milliliters (ml)
Fluid ounces (fl oz)	29.57	Milliliters (ml)
Cups (c)	236.59	Milliliters (ml)
Cups (c)	0.236	Liters (l)
Pints (pt)	473.18	Milliliters (ml)
Pints (pt)	0.473	Liters (l)
Quarts (qt)	946.36	Milliliters (ml)
Quarts (qt)	0.946	Liters (l)
Gallons (gal)	3.785	Liters (l)
Ounces (oz)	28.35	Grams (g)
Pounds (lbs)	0.454	Kilograms (kg)
Inches (in; ")	2.54	Centimeters (cm)

temperatures

To convert Fahrenheit (US) to Celsius:
Fahrenheit temperature - (minus) 32 x (multiplied by) 5, then / (divided by) 9 = Celsius temperature

FAHRENHEIT	CELSIUS
250°	120°
275°	140°
300°	150°
325°	160°
350°	180°
375°	190°
400°	200°
425°	220°
450°	230°

quick reference

US MEASUREMENT	METRIC MEASUREMENT
1 fl oz	29.6 ml
1/4 tsp	1.23 ml
1/2 tbsp	2.46 ml
3/4 tbsp	3.7 ml
1 tsp	4.93 ml
1 1/4 tsp	6.16 ml
1 1/2 tsp	7.39 ml
1 3/4 tsp	8.63 ml
2 tsp	9.86 ml
1 tbsp	14.79 ml
2 tbsp	29.57 ml
1/4 c	59.15 ml
1/2 c	118.3 ml
1 c (8oz)	236.59 ml
2 c or 1 pt	473.18 ml
3 c	709.77 ml
4 c or 1 qt (32oz)	946.36 ml
4 qt or 1 gal	3.785 l

Dear Guests,
Please help yourselves
to cake and coffee.

the
projects

The projects in this book are broken into three sections, organized by the type of icing used: buttercream, chocolate and fondant. The different types of icing give the cakes distinctive appearances and use specific techniques, which are explained in detail at the beginning of each section. Be sure to read these explanations before you begin the decorating process so that you have as much information as possible. Other techniques, like making royal icing flowers and decorations, are woven throughout all the sections.

The cakes in each section range from quick and easy to a bit more elaborate. The simple design of The Dots (page 38) will allow you to bake, decorate and enjoy the cake all in an afternoon. You may need to spend a little more time, however, crafting the royal icing decorations for Springtime Garden (page 50) and Bugs and Bees (page 86).

In this book, you will find many decorating techniques for a wide variety of projects. Every cake can be adapted to suit any number of guests or special occasion. Adding a "Happy Birthday" or "Congratulations" message on the cake will make it even more personal. I purposefully did not include wedding cakes in this book, as they have their own specific techniques and needs. Many of the cakes, such as Lily of the Valley, can be made into stacked wedding cakes if you desire (see page 63).

The Beautifully Buttercream section features six delicious projects. The Festive Yule Log (page 64) differs from the other cakes as it is covered in chocolate buttercream instead of regular buttercream. It is one of my standard cakes during the holiday season and is always a huge success.

The four projects in the Creations in Chocolate section will satisfy any chocolate-lover's craving. You will find that I don't use traditional chocolate techniques like tempering, as they are time-consuming and drive me crazy! I also make chocolate leaves with cookie cutters instead of hand-shaping them because it is much easier and more fun.

I used a variety of creative themes for the five cakes in the Fancy in Fondant section, from flowers and fruit to hearts and holidays. Fondant's appearance is a sure crowd-pleaser, however its bland taste is not always so well-received. A bit of clear flavoring or liqueur makes it just as pleasing to the palette as it is to the eye.

beautifully
buttercream

Buttercream icing is very popular because it is easy to use and it tastes great! Buttercream is ideal for icing cakes to a smooth finish, as well as piping flowers and cake borders.

The projects in this chapter all begin with cakes covered in buttercream icing. Some must be crumb-coated (see page 20) and are then covered in berries, chocolate shavings or royal icing flowers. Others must be iced to a smooth finish (see page 38, steps 1 to 3).

To crumb-coat an 8" round cake, you will need about two cups (16oz) of icing, which is ½ the quantity of the classic buttercream icing recipe from page 30. To ice an 8" (20cm) round cake to a smooth finish, you will also need about two cups (16oz) of icing. I usually start with three cups (24oz), and as I work the excess icing off the edges, I am left with enough extra icing for filling and decorating. Keep in mind that these measurements are only approximate. You may wish to use more or less icing depending on your taste.

the
dots

This is a quick and easy cake that will give you stunning results. Bright colors combined with simple elegance make it one of my favorites. The piping is easy to do and perfect for beginners, and the color palette can be adjusted to your specifications.

Ingredients You'll Need:

8" (20cm) round cake crumb-coated with classic buttercream icing (see page 20)

¾ quantity classic buttercream icing (recipe on page 30)

Supplies You'll Need:

Red gerbera daisy

⁹⁄₁₆" (1.4cm) wide red satin floral ribbon

¹⁵⁄₁₆" (3cm) wide orange satin floral ribbon

Cloth pastry bag

Tip: #4

Spatula

Cake scraper

Turntable

Serving platter

1. Cover Cake with Icing

Place a crumb-coated cake on a turntable and spoon a large amount of buttercream icing onto the top. Work the icing over the sides and top with a spatula.

2. Smooth Icing

Dip a cake scraper into warm water and use it to smooth the sides of the cake, rotating the turntable and leaving the scraper stationary. The warm water will melt the icing, giving it a smooth finish. Dip the scraper back into the warm water as necessary. Work excess icing from the edges of the cake in toward the center with a spatula. Scrape the excess icing onto the side of a bowl.

3. Smooth Cake

Dip the spatula in warm water and use it to smooth the top of the cake.

4. Pipe Dots

Fill a pastry bag with the remaining buttercream icing from step 2. Using tip #4, pipe small dots randomly over the entire cake. Press each dot lightly with your finger to remove peaks made by the tip.

5. Pipe Bottom Border

Using the same tip and icing, pipe a thin line around the bottom of the cake, rotating the turntable as necessary. Don't worry if it isn't perfect. It will just be used to secure the ribbon.

6. Add Ribbons

Cut the orange and red floral ribbons to the diameter of the cake. Wrap the orange ribbon around the bottom of the cake and press lightly against the line of icing to adhere. Add a small drop of icing to the end of the ribbon to secure. Wrap the red ribbon around the orange ribbon and dot with icing to adhere.

7. Add Daisy

Add a red gerbera daisy to the top of the cake and use icing to secure. Transfer to a serving platter.

variation

Changing the color of the ribbons and type of flowers on this cake will create a totally different mood. Match the decorations to the color scheme of any event!

lace and roses

This is an elegant cake for any occasion. Sugarcoating the roses gives them a softer appearance and allows them to last much longer. Cornelli, which is a continuous squiggly line of icing, is easy to master, and the white color makes a nice contrast against the cake, which is covered in classic buttercream icing tinted a soft yellow.

Ingredients You'll Need:

8" (20cm) round cake covered to a smooth finish with classic buttercream icing tinted soft yellow (see page 40, steps 1 to 3)

3⁄8 quantity classic buttercream icing (recipe on page 30)

1⁄4 cup (50g) granulated sugar

Egg whites

Supplies You'll Need:

Yellow rose with pink tips

Cloth pastry bag

Tips: #2 and 12

Pastry brush

Small bowl

Small plate

Turntable

Serving platter

2. Sugarcoat Petals and Rosebud

Pour the sugar onto a small plate. Coat the petals and rosebud with the sugar and shake off the excess. Set aside to dry.

1. Prepare Rose

Add the egg whites to a small bowl. Remove four or five petals from a rose and use a pastry brush to cover each petal with egg whites. Brush the rosebud with egg whites as well.

3. Pipe Cornelli

Place the soft yellow buttercream-coated cake on the turntable. Fill a pastry bag with classic butter-cream icing and use tip #2 to pipe thin, squiggly lines of cornelli over the entire cake. Rotate the turntable as you go.

4. Pipe Pearl Border

Transfer the cake to a serving platter. Place tip #12 on the pastry bag and pipe a pearl border of classic buttercream icing along the bottom edge of the cake. To do this, squeeze out a dot resembling a pearl, then move the tip backward to taper the pearl. Move the pastry bag forward again to make the next pearl, and so on.

5. Arrange on Cake

Add the sugarcoated rosebud and petals to the top of the cake as desired.

the language OF FLOWERS

Flowers not only make beautiful cake decorations, but they also send messages of gratitude, luck, friendship and love. The language of flowers, called "floriography," can help you communicate your message. Here are a few of my favorite flowers and their meanings:

Daisy: Innocence, romance

Geranium: Peace of mind

Lily of the Valley: Purity, return of happiness

Pansy: Pleasant thoughts

Orchid: Love and beauty

Poppy: Flirtation, dreaminess

Rose (pink): Secret love, sweetness

Rose (red): Romantic love

Rose (white): Innocent love

Rose (wild): Simplicity

Rose (yellow/peach/orange): Friendship

Sunflower: You are splendid

Violet: Faithfulness, loyalty

fresh flower
basket

The basket weave design requires a little more patience and time, but it will make an impressive display. Use your favorite flowers in any color combination to create a look all your own.

Ingredients You'll Need:

8" (20cm) round cake crumb-coated with classic buttercream icing (see page 20)

½ quantity classic buttercream icing (recipe on page 30)

Supplies You'll Need:

Fresh flowers and greenery

Cloth pastry bag

Tips: #7 and 67

Turntable

Serving platter

1. Pipe Upward Strokes

Place the crumb-coated cake on the turntable. Fill the pastry bag with classic buttercream icing. Using tip #7, pipe vertical lines in upward strokes all the way around the cake, spacing them about ½" (1.3cm) apart.

2. Pipe Horizontal Lines

Using tip #67, pipe a horizontal line to cover one of the vertical lines at the base of the cake. Skip one line, cover the following line, and so on. Moving upward on your next pass around the cake, cover the lines that were skipped during the first pass. Continue upward until the sides are completely covered. This will form a basket weave appearance.

3. Pipe Top Border

Use tip #67 to pipe a border around the top of the cake. To do this, make a wave motion back and forth with the pastry bag.

4. Add Greenery

Arrange greenery randomly around the top of the cake, leaving space in the middle for fresh flowers.

5. Add Flowers

Randomly add fresh flowers to the top of the cake.

6. Add More Greenery

Add finishing touches of flowers and greenery for a well-decorated cake. Transfer to a serving platter.

variation

Change the look of this cake by choosing flowers in different colors. Pastel colors are especially beautiful in early spring.

springtime
garden

Lots of different techniques are used in this cake. I used a combination of buttercream icing and royal icing to make the flowers and leaves. The white chocolate shavings and ganache also add a special sweetness to this cake. Don't let the number of steps intimidate you. Royal icing flowers and chocolate shavings can be made up to several months ahead of time and kept in sealed containers until you need them.

*Since more than one color and type
of icing are needed for this project,
I recommend using several pastry bags.

Ingredients You'll Need:

8" (20cm) round cake crumb-coated
with classic buttercream icing
(see page 20)

1 quantity royal icing divided into ⅓ red;
⅓ yellow; ⅓ white (recipe on page 32)

½ quantity classic buttercream icing
divided into ½ white; ⅓ green; ⅙ pink
(recipe on page 30)

¾ quantity white chocolate ganache
(recipe on page 31)

6 ounces (170g) white chocolate, melted

Supplies You'll Need:

Flower nail

Parchment paper cut into small squares

Cookie sheet

Cloth pastry bags*

Tips: #2, 3, 4, 13, 61, 67, 101, 103
and 199

Food coloring paste: burgundy and
yellow

Small paintbrush

Two small bowls

Cutting board

Spatula

Large straight edge knife

Turntable

Serving platter

1. Prepare Flower Nail

Fill a pastry bag with red royal icing. Using tip #61, apply a dot of royal icing to a flower nail and stick a small square of parchment paper to the icing. The icing will hold the parchment paper in place.

2. Make Geranium Petals

To make the geraniums, hold the wide end of tip #61 on the parchment paper and squeeze out the icing as you rotate the nail one-fourth of a turn.

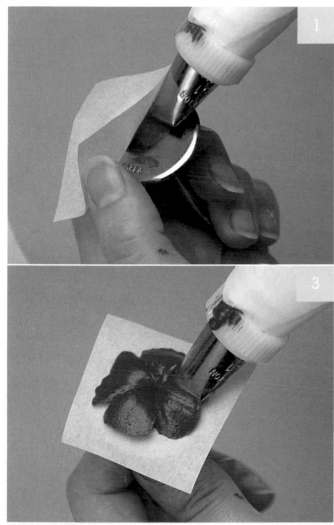

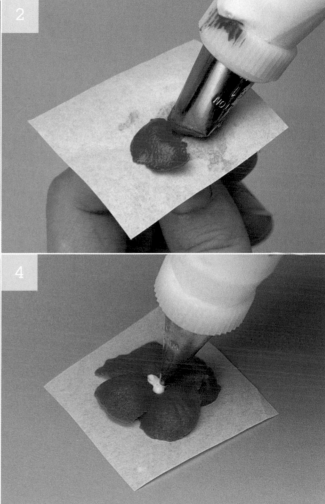

3. Make Four More Petals

Repeat step 2 to make three additional petals. Remove the parchment paper from the flower nail and place it on a cookie sheet. Repeat this process to make the desired number of geraniums for the cake.

4. Pipe Flower Centers

Fill a pastry bag with yellow royal icing. Using tip #2, pipe four small dots in the center of each geranium. Allow the flowers to dry overnight.

5. Make Bottom Pansy Petal

To make the pansies, fill a pastry bag with white royal icing and prepare the flower nail with parchment paper as shown in step 1. Use tip #103 to pipe a large bottom petal by holding the wide end of the tip down on the nail. Rotate the nail in one-half of a turn.

6. Make Side Petals

Make two small, round side petals by holding the wide end of the tip toward the middle of the flower. The thin end will point toward the outside of the flower to make a thin edge. Keep the nail stationary and make a dollop.

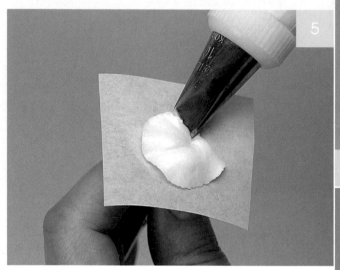

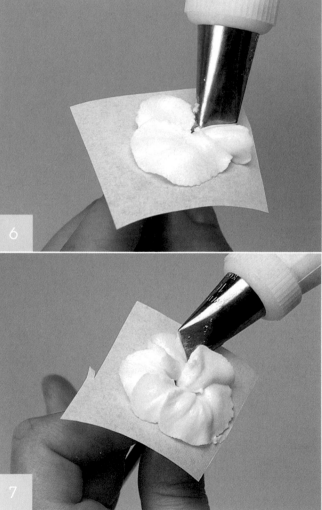

7. Make Top Petals

Make the top two petals in the same manner as you made the side petals. Remove the parchment paper from the nail and place it on a cookie sheet. Repeat this process to make the desired number of pansies for the cake.

8. Pipe Pansy Centers

Fill a pastry bag with yellow royal icing. Using tip #3, pipe three small dots in the center of each pansy. Allow the flowers to dry overnight.

9. Pipe Drop Flowers

To make drop flowers, place tip #4 on the pastry bag filled with white royal icing. Make five small dots in a circle on a cookie sheet lined with parchment paper. Repeat this process until you have made the desired number of drop flowers. Place tip #13 on the pastry bag filled with yellow royal icing make small star centers. Allow the flowers to dry overnight.

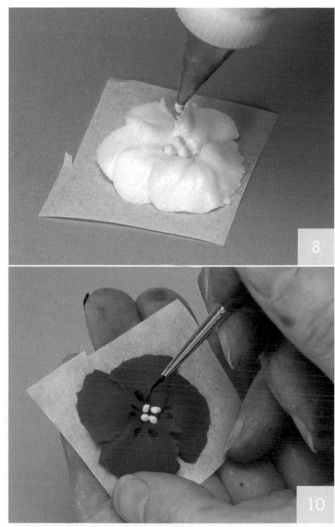

10. Paint Geranium Details

When the geraniums are dry and hard, dip a small paintbrush in burgundy food coloring paste and paint two lines on each geranium petal. Set aside to dry.

11. Paint Pansy Details

When the pansies are dry and hard, dip a small paintbrush in yellow food coloring paste and paint three to five lines on the bottom petal of each pansy. Set aside to dry.

tasty
TIDBIT You can tell
chocolate is hard
when it has lost its sheen.

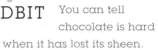

12. Make White Chocolate Shavings

Pour the melted white chocolate onto a cutting board or hard surface.

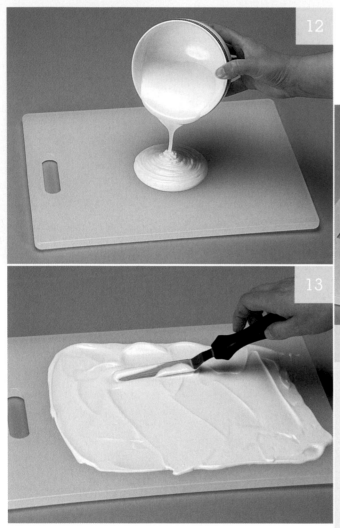

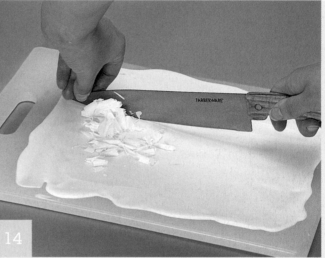

14. Scrape Off Layers

Use a large straight edge knife to scrape off layers of white chocolate to form shavings. For white chocolate curls, scrape off longer layers.

13. Spread Chocolate and Cool

Spread the white chocolate evenly to about ⅛" (0.3cm) thickness with a spatula. Leave the white chocolate at room temperature until it has hardened. For quick hardening, refrigerate for 10 minutes.

15. Coat Cake with Shavings

Hold the bottom of the freshly crumb-coated cake with one hand and press the white chocolate shavings into the sides of the cake with the other. Be sure the cake is freshly coated. Otherwise, the shavings won't stick to the cake.

16. Spread Ganache

Transfer the cake to a turntable. Pour white chocolate ganache over the top of the cake and spread it with a spatula. Do not spread the ganache all the way to the edge or it will run down the sides and ruin your shavings. Refrigerate for about 15 minutes to allow the ganache to set.

17. Make Border

When the ganache has set, use a pastry bag filled with white buttercream icing and tip #199 to make a spiral border. Do do this, move the pastry bag clockwise in a spiral, then counterclockwise in a spiral, all the way around the top edge of the cake.

18. Pipe Vines on Cake

Use a pastry bag filled with green buttercream icing and tip #4 to pipe vines on the top of the cake.

tasty

TIDBIT   If you are unsure about where to place your vines, score them on the cake with a toothpick first.

19. Pipe Leaves onto Vines

Place tip #67 on the bag with the green buttercream icing and pipe leaves onto the vines. Arrange the royal icing pansies, geraniums and drop flowers on the vines on top of the cake.

21. Add Tendrils

Place tip #2 on the pastry bag with green buttercream icing and squeeze the bag tightly so that the icing curls to make tendrils. Transfer the cake to a serving platter.

20. Pipe Mini-Roses

Fill a pastry bag with pink buttercream icing and use tip #101 to pipe mini-roses onto the vines. To do this, hold the pastry bag with the wider edge of the tip on the cake and the thin edge pointing up. Move the bag straight up, then to the left and right.

lily of the valley

I love the effect the Lily of the Valley makes on this cake. The royal icing flowers and leaves, which appear to be sprouting from the cake, are quite simple to make. I recommend making them at least a day ahead of time so they have plenty of time to dry.

Ingredients You'll Need:

8" (20cm) round cake covered to a smooth finish with classic buttercream icing (see page 40, steps 1 to 3)

1 quantity royal icing divided into ⅔ green; ⅓ white (recipe on page 32)

¾ quantity classic buttercream icing divided into ½ green; ½ white (recipe on page 30)

Supplies You'll Need:

24- or 26-gauge floral wire

Styrofoam

Cloth pastry bags*

Tips: #4, 7, 103 and 104

Turntable

Serving platter

*Since more than one color and type of icing are needed for this project, I recommend using several pastry bags.

1. Pipe Lily Leaves

To make the leaves for this cake, fill a pastry bag with green royal icing and add tip #104. Cut three to five pieces of floral wire about 5" (13cm) long and gently curve them with your fingers. Stick the end of one of the wires two-thirds of the way into the pastry bag.

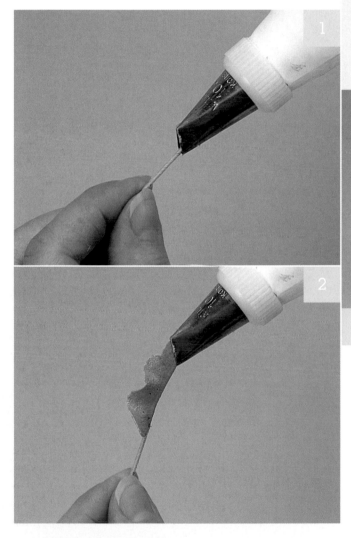

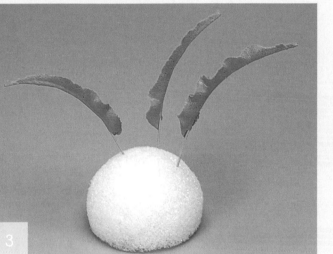

3. Dry Leaves Upright

To dry the leaves upright, stick the wire stems into a piece of Styrofoam.

2. Make More Leaves

Squeeze the bag as you pull out the wire to make a thin leaf. Repeat this process to make the remainder of the leaves.

4. Pipe Flowers

To pipe the flowers, fill a pastry bag with white royal icing and add tip #4. Cut five to seven pieces of floral wire about 5" (13cm) long and bend them into candy cane shapes. Pipe four to five small dots of icing onto each stem, starting at the tip and working down the underside of the stem. Stick the stems into the foam and allow to dry.

5. Arrange Flowers and Leaves

Place the buttercream-coated cake on the turntable. Once the leaves and flowers are hard, arrange them in an off-center bouquet on top of the cake.

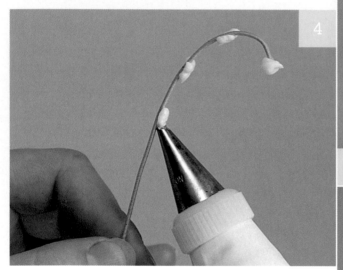

6. Pipe Stems on Cake

Fill a pastry bag with green buttercream icing. Using tip #4, pipe stems randomly onto the top and sides of the cake, rotating the turntable as necessary.

7. Pipe Flowers on Stems

Fill a pastry bag with white buttercream icing. Use tip #7 to pipe small dots onto the stems as flowers.

9. Pipe Ruffled Border

Transfer the cake to a serving platter. Place tip #104 on the pastry bag filled with white buttercream icing and pipe a white ruffled border around the bottom. To do this, hold the thick edge of the tip against the bottom of the cake and the platter. Go around twice, with the second ruffled layer on top of the first one.

8. Pipe Leaves

Place tip #103 on the pastry bag filled with green buttercream icing. Pipe leaves onto the cake, holding the thin edge away from the cake with the thick edge pointing downward.

variation

This cake, like many in this book, can easily be adapted into a stacked or tiered cake for a wedding reception or large gathering. Stacked cakes, like the one shown here, are set one on top of the other, and each layer is supported by plastic or wooden sticks hidden in the cakes. Tiered cakes are also stacked vertically, but each layer is separated by a support structure like small pillars on top of the layers.

a wedding cake TRADITION

Some newlyweds follow the tradition of saving the top tier of their wedding cake to eat on their first anniversary. While eating anything that has been frozen for a year may not sound appetizing, your cake will taste almost as delicious as it did on your wedding day if you follow these simple steps:

1. Remove the cake topper, flowers and other inedible decorations from the top tier of the cake.

2. Store the cake in the freezer until it is frozen solid (about three hours).

3. Cover the frozen cake in a layer of plastic wrap and then in a layer of aluminum foil.

4. Place the cake in an airtight container to prevent freezer burn.

5. Store in the back of the freezer until your first anniversary.

6. To thaw, remove the cake from the container but do not remove the foil and plastic wrap. (The wrap will collect the condensation rather than the cake.)

7. Allow the cake to sit at room temperature for at least 12 hours.

8. Remove the foil and plastic wrap from the cake and enjoy!

NOTE: Once the cake has thawed, it should not be re-frozen.

festive
yule log

Always a huge hit during the holiday season, this festive cake tends to steal the show! The cake roll in this project must be made ahead of time so that it has plenty of time to set. Add the finishing touches right before it is served. That way, you'll enjoy the party instead of spending all of your time in the kitchen.

*Since more than one color and type of icing are needed for this project, I recommend using several pastry bags.

Ingredients You'll Need:

Sheet cake baked on a 9" x 13" (23cm x 33cm) cookie sheet, uniced

2 quantities royal icing divided into ⅝ green; ⅛ red; ⅛ yellow; ⅛ white (recipe on page 32)

⅛ quantity classic buttercream icing (recipe on page 30)

⅔ quantity chocolate buttercream icing (recipe on page 31)

White chocolate curls and shavings (see page 55)

Chocolate syrup (any store-bought brand will work)

1 pint (473ml) vanilla ice cream, softened

Water

Supplies You'll Need:

Trees and Leaves pattern (page 73)

Foil-covered cardboard

Cloth pastry bags*

Tips: #2, 4, 16 and any small star tip

Food coloring paste: green, red and black

Paintbrush

Small bowl

Parchment paper

Cutting board

Clear tape

Spatula

Large straight edge knife

Fork

Turntable

Serving platter

1. Prepare Pattern

Make a copy of the Trees and Leaves pattern on page 73. Enlarge the pattern if you would like to make bigger decorations. Place the pattern on a cookie sheet and cover it with parchment paper so that the designs are visible through the paper. Tape the sides down to prevent slippage.

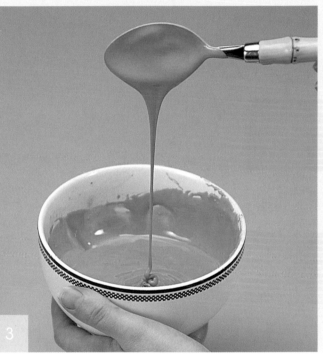

2. Trace Shapes

Fill a pastry bag with green royal icing and use tip #4 to trace the outline of the shapes.

3. Thin Icing

Empty the remaining icing from the pastry bag into a small bowl. Add small amounts of water slowly and mix. Add more water as necessary until the consistency is runny but not watery. The icing should still coat the spoon and run off to form a ribbon.

4. Fill Outlines

Pour the thinned icing back into the pastry bag and fill in the outlines of the trees and leaves. The harder icing works as a barrier for the softer icing to keep it from spreading. This is called "flooding."

5. Pipe Berries

Fill a pastry bag with red royal icing and use tip #2 to pipe dots onto the parchment paper for berries.

6. Add Stars to Berries

Push into each berry with a small star tip before it is fully dry. Set the decorations aside to harden.

7. Pipe Ornaments on Trees

Once the royal icing decorations have hardened, use the pastry bag filled with red royal icing to make small ornaments on some of the trees.

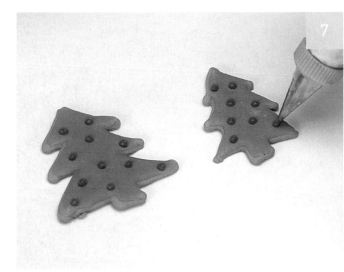

8. Pipe Swags

Add a small amount of white royal icing to a pastry bag, and using tip #2, drag the tip across some of the trees to make swags.

9. Pipe Stars

Add a small amount of yellow royal icing to a pastry bag and use tip #16 to make stars on the tops of each tree.

10. Paint Details on Icing

Dip a small paintbrush in green food coloring paste and paint veins onto each leaf. Paint the indentations on the berries with black food coloring paste. Set all the royal icing decorations aside to dry.

tasty

TIDBIT A freshly baked cake is much easier to roll because it is moist, and less likely to break or crumble. Make sure it is cool, however, or it will melt the ice cream.

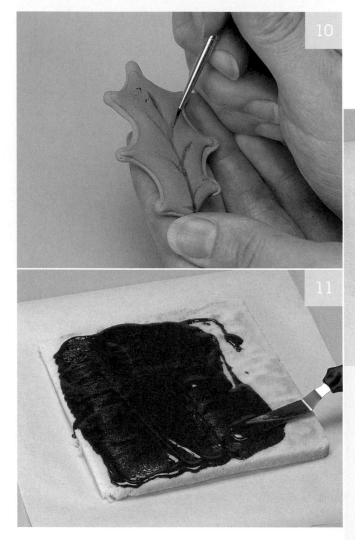

12. Add Vanilla Ice Cream

Spread softened vanilla ice cream over one half of the cake and smooth it out quickly with a spatula.

11. Syrup the Cake

Trim the sides of a freshly baked sheet cake to make them straight and place it on a sheet of parchment paper. Pour chocolate syrup over the cake and spread it with a spatula.

tasty
TIDBIT I recommend preparing
the cake and decorations
a few days—or even a week—
ahead of time. They will have
plenty of time to set, and you
can add the finishing touches
right before it is served.

14. Continue Rolling

Continue to roll the cake, lifting the parchment paper to help it along. Don't be discouraged if the cake breaks and crumbles. It will be covered in icing later.

13. Begin Rolling Cake

Lift the end of the cake covered in ice cream to start making a roll.

15. Finish Roll and Freeze

Complete the roll and shape it with the parchment paper to resemble a log. Fold the ends of the paper in to completely wrap the log. Freeze for at least four hours.

16. Slice Log

After the cake log has set, remove it from the freezer and peel off the parchment paper. Place the log on a cutting board and cut a 1" (2.5cm) "stump" from one end with a large straight edge knife.

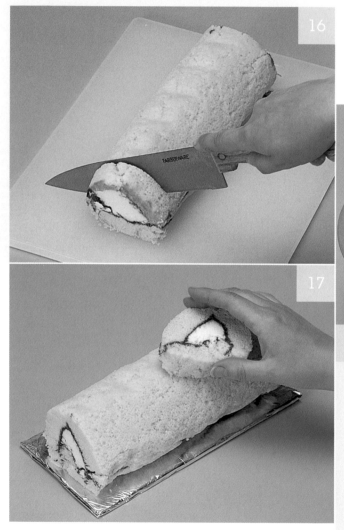

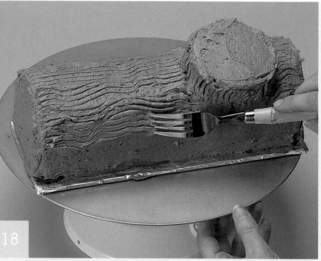

18. Cover with Icing

Place the cake and foil base on the turntable. Cover the entire cake with chocolate buttercream icing, rotating the turntable as you go. Work quickly so that the ice cream doesn't melt. Add texture lines by dragging a fork horizontally across the buttercream. Return the cake to the freezer for a few hours to set.

17. Transfer Log and Add Stump

Transfer the log to the foil-covered cardboard and position the stump on top of the log near one end. If the ice cream is melting as you work, return the log to the freezer until it is frozen again.

19. Pipe Spirals

Remove the cake from the freezer once it has had time to set. Add classic buttercream icing to a pastry bag and use tip #4 to pipe spirals on the ends of the log and stump.

21. Add Shavings

As a finishing touch, add white chocolate curls and shavings for snow. (For instructions, see page 55.)

20. Add Decorations

Transfer the cake and foil base to a serving platter and add the royal icing decorations. It is important that you add them just before serving. Otherwise, condensation will form on the icing as it thaws, which may cause it to melt.

Use this Trees and Leaves pattern at actual size, or enlarge it on a duplicating machine for larger decorations.

tasty

TIDBIT Use the flooding technique to make royal icing decorations in all shapes, sizes and colors. Simply draw the desired shape on a piece of paper, place a sheet of parchment paper over it so that the drawing shows through, outline the shape with colored royal icing and flood the icing. Once the decorations have hardened, they can be added to your cake!

creations in
chocolate

The most important thing to remember when working with chocolate is to lick your fingers often! There are also a few important rules you should follow when handling chocolate.

First, you must understand the difference between real chocolate and candy melt or bark covering. Real chocolate (dark, milk and white) contains cocoa butter, while candy melt or bark covering contains chocolate "flavoring." I prefer to use real chocolate, like semi-sweet chocolate chips, when making ganache (recipe on page 31).

For decorations, however, I prefer chocolate candy melt. It is more stable since it doesn't contain cocoa butter. When real chocolate is melted, it must be tempered, or heated to a certain temperature, then cooled for a period of time. Otherwise, it will turn white, lose its sheen and even become soft and change its consistency altogether. The tempering process takes time and patience, and therefore candy melt is a good alternative!

The easiest way to melt chocolate or candy melt is in the microwave. Place the chocolate in a plastic bowl and melt it in short bursts of about 25 to 35 seconds at half power. Be sure to stir the chocolate between each burst. It should be warm, but never hot to the touch. Once chocolate is burned, it cannot be saved.

The biggest enemy of chocolate is water. Always be sure that the bowls and spoons you use are completely dry. Even a few drops of water can ruin the chocolate, making it curdle or turning it into a paste that will not set up even when it is cooled.

The chocolate decorations in the projects that follow, such as the leaves and filigrees, can be made ahead of time if desired. Just be sure to store them in a cool room with low humidity to preserve their appearance.

double chocolate
delight

This delicious cake will tempt the taste buds of any chocolate lover. The white chocolate filigrees add pizzazz to this dark chocolate confection. Use chocolate buttercream to fill the cake, or try whipped ganache for a richer taste.

Ingredients You'll Need:

9" (23cm) round chocolate cake crumb-coated with chocolate buttercream icing (see page 20)

⅕ quantity chocolate buttercream icing (recipe on page 31)

1¾ quantities dark chocolate ganache (recipe on page 31)

⅓ quantity white chocolate ganache (recipe on page 31)

Milk chocolate ganache (mix slightly less than 4 tbsp (60ml) white chocolate ganache and 1 tbsp (15ml) dark chocolate ganache)

4 ounces (113g) white chocolate, melted

Supplies You'll Need:

Three homemade pastry bags (see page 23)

Cloth pastry bag

Tip: #114

Cookie sheet

Parchment paper

Spatula

Straight edge knife

Turntable

Serving platter

1. Create Filigrees

To create the filigree decorations for this cake, pour melted white chocolate into a homemade pastry bag. Drizzle the white chocolate onto a cookie sheet lined with parchment paper. Work quickly in one diagonal direction, then the other, then up and down. Fold the bag to squeeze out more chocolate. Set the filigrees aside to harden, or refrigerate for quick set-up.

2. Add Ganache

Place the crumb-coated cake on the turntable. Pour dark chocolate ganache over the top and allow it to run down the sides while you smooth the top with a spatula. Work the spatula around the sides, rotating the turntable as you go.

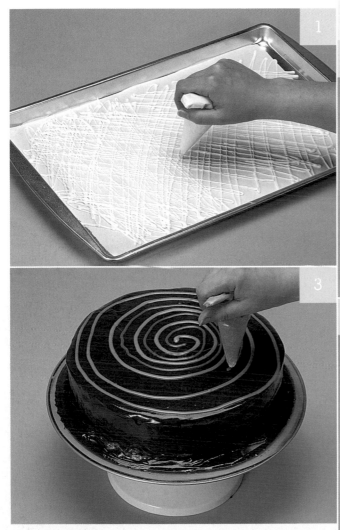

3. Pipe Spiral

Fill homemade pastry bags with melted white and milk chocolate ganache before starting the icing process. Ganache sets up quickly, so you need to work fast. Use the bag filled with white chocolate ganache to pipe a spiral on the top of the cake. Use the bag filled with milk chocolate ganache to pipe a second spiral between the lines of the white chocolate spiral.

4. Create Feathering

Drag a straight edge knife from the center to the outside of the cake, then back to the center.

tasty
TIDBIT
White chocolate decorations can be stored in a container at room temperature for several weeks. No refrigeration is necessary.

5. Transfer to Serving Platter

Carefully transfer the cake to a serving platter and clean up the excess ganache at the bottom with a damp towel.

6. Add Filigrees

Break off small pieces of filigree from step 1 and arrange them around the base of the cake. Press gently to adhere to the icing. Refrigerate for several hours to allow the cake to set.

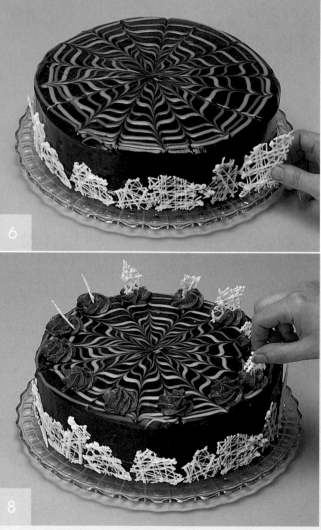

7. Pipe Rosettes

Remove the cake from the refrigerator once it is set. Fill a cloth pastry bag with chocolate buttercream icing and use tip #114 to pipe rosettes around the edges of the cake. To do this, hold the bag upright and pipe in a circular motion to form peaked swirls.

8. Add More Filigrees

Break off small pieces of filigree and stick one into each rosette.

white chocolate
berry fantasy

This is one of my favorite cakes. I like the bright colors of the berries and ribbon together. I recommend using whipped cream as a filling and adding some berries to the inside of the cake as well. Whipped cream, white chocolate and berries are just delicious!

Ingredients You'll Need:

8" (20cm) square cake crumb-coated with classic buttercream icing (see page 20)

16 ounces (454g) white chocolate, melted

1 basket each of strawberries, blueberries, blackberries and raspberries

Supplies You'll Need:

⁵⁄₁₆"(0.8cm) wide satin floral ribbon in various colors

Cookie sheet

Metal ruler

Parchment paper

Straight edge knife

Scissors

Serving platter

2. Measure Cake Dimensions

Place the crumb-coated cake on a serving platter.
Measure the width and height of the cake, and add
1/8" (0.5cm) to the height. For example, the cake
in this project measures 7⁹⁄₁₆" (20cm) in width and
4" (10cm) in height , so my measurements will
be 7⁹⁄₁₆" x 4¹⁄₈" (20cm x 10.5cm).

1. Make Chocolate Shells

Pour melted white chocolate evenly on a cookie
sheet lined with parchment paper. To ensure that the
chocolate is even, shake the cookie sheet from side
to side and front to back. Set it aside until the
chocolate is almost completely hardened. This will be
the shell that covers the sides of the cake.

3. Mark Measurements and Score Chocolate

Mark the cake measurements on your hardening
white chocolate sheet and score the chocolate with a
straight edge knife. After it is scored, set it aside to
harden completely.

4. Peel Chocolate Sheets from Paper

When the white chocolate has hardened completely, run a straight edge knife lightly over the score marks several times, cutting deeper with each pass. Run the knife around the edges of the pan. Slowly peel the chocolate from the paper and carefully break along the score marks. Save the excess white chocolate for later.

tasty
TIDBIT Be sure the white chocolate is cut all the way through before removing it from the paper.

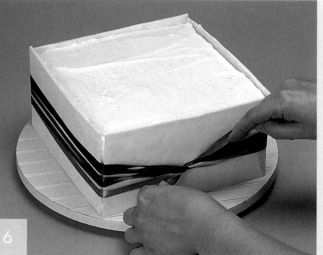

6. Add Ribbons

Cut several colorful ribbons and wrap them around the sides of the cake. Tie into a double knot.

5. Press Sheets Against Cake Sides

Gently press the white chocolate sheets against each side of the cake to adhere them to the icing. Do not press too hard or they will break.

7. Arrange Ribbons and Tie Bow

Separate the ribbons so that each color rests flat against the cake. Tie the ribbons into a large bow and trim the ends at an angle.

9. Add Chocolate Shards

Cut or break the leftover white chocolate pieces from step 4 into pointy shards. Position them at the back corner of the cake.

8. Add Berries

Arrange the strawberries, blueberries, blackberries and raspberries on top of the cake.

variations

Berries are great cake decorations because they do not turn brown when exposed to the air. Try substituting dark chocolate with cherries (above) or milk chocolate with strawberries (right) for a tasty variation.

bugs and bees

These whimsical cakes are great for parties. They are elegant enough for afternoon tea, yet fun enough for a child's birthday. Save time by making the royal icing bugs and bees in advance. They last for months in an airtight container.

Ingredients You'll Need:

Sheet cake baked on a 9" x 13" (23cm x 33cm) cookie sheet, uniced

1½ quantities royal icing divided into ⅓ red; ⅓ yellow; ⅙ white; ⅙ black (recipe on page 32)

⅘ quantity chocolate buttercream icing (recipe on page 31)

3¼ quantities dark chocolate ganache (recipe on page 31)

1 quantity sugar syrup (recipe on page 30)

Supplies You'll Need:

Cloth pastry bags*

Tips: #1, 4, 12 and 104

Cookie sheet

Wire rack

Cutting board

Ruler

Parchment paper

Spatula

Serrated knife

Straight edge knife

*Since more than one color and type of icing are needed for this project, I recommend using several pastry bags.

2. Pipe Bee Bodies

Fill a pastry bag with yellow royal icing.
Use tip #12 to pipe longer bodies for the bees.

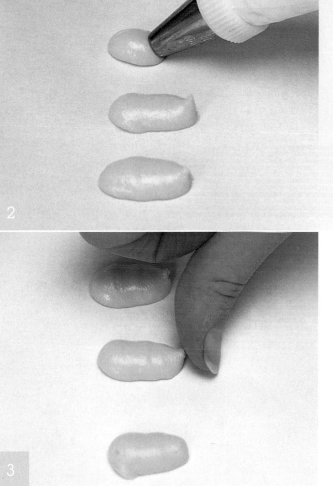

1. Pipe Bug Bodies

Line a cookie sheet with parchment paper. Fill a pastry bag with red royal icing and insert tip #12. Hold the pastry bag at a 45° angle and pull it toward you, piping several round ladybug bodies onto the parchment paper.

3. Smooth Pointy Edges

As the bodies dry, press in the pointy edges with your thumb to smooth.

4. Pipe Bug Heads

Fill a pastry bag with black royal icing and insert tip #4. Pipe a small sideways oval on one end of each ladybug body. This becomes the head.

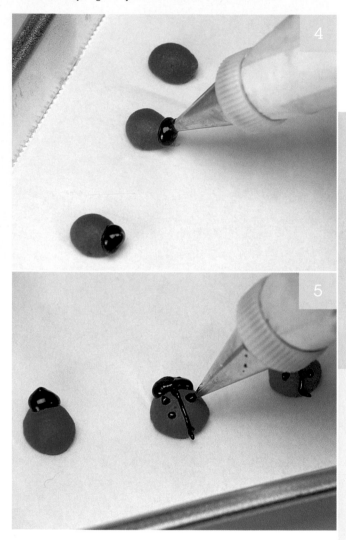

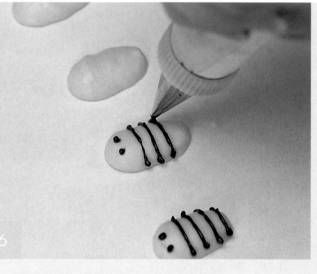

6. Pipe Bee Details

Using the same black royal icing and tip #1, pipe two dots for eyes on the bees' heads and three or four stripes across the bees' bodies.

5. Pipe Bug Details

Using the same black royal icing and tip #1, pipe a line through the middle and two or three dots on each side of the ladybug bodies.

tasty

TIDBIT For clean edges
when trimming the
edges of a cake, wipe the
knife with a warm, wet
washcloth between cuts.

8. Prepare Cake

Cut the sheet cake into two pieces, coat each
piece with sugar syrup and cover the top of one
piece with chocolate buttercream icing. Stack
the uncovered piece on top of the covered piece.
Freeze the cake overnight so that it is easier to
handle. Transfer the frozen cake to a cutting board
and use a serrated knife to cut the edges off of the
sides of the cake as shown. This will make the sides
straight up and down.

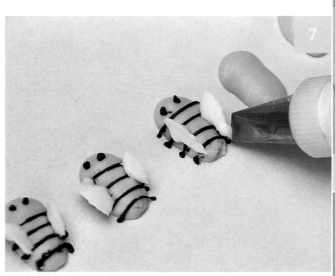

7. Pipe Bees' Wings

Fill a pastry bag with white royal icing and insert
tip #104 to make the wings. Hold the bag at a
45° angle with the thin end on top and pull it toward
you. Set the cookie sheet of bugs and bees aside to
harden.

9. Slice Cake into Bars

Score the cake into even bars using the tip of a
sharp, straight edge knife. Use a ruler as a guide if
necessary. The bars in this project measure 1¼" x
3½" (3cm x 9cm). Cut along the score marks.

10. Spread Ganache

Transfer the cake bars to a wire rack with a cookie sheet underneath. Pour dark chocolate ganache onto the top of each bar and spread with a spatula. The cookie sheet will catch any drippings.

11. Add Bugs and Bees

Arrange the royal icing bugs and bees on the top and sides of the cake bars as desired.

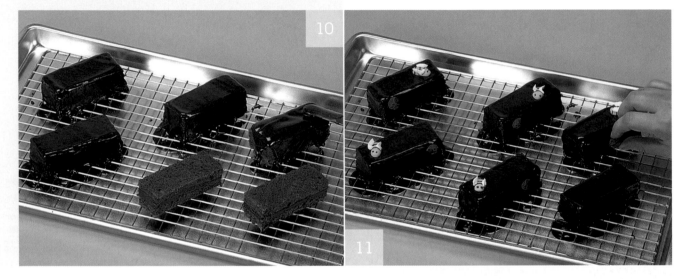

variation

These small, elegant cakes are covered in white chocolate ganache. I made the flowers with royal icing and pipe leaves and stems with green buttercream icing.

chocolate
fall cake

Believe it or not, this is one of the most forgiving cakes in the book. The technique is surprisingly easy and will leave your guests awed. Trying to guess how you could have possibly made it will be the subject of discussion for the evening! Feel free to replace the leaves with any other shapes to go with the season.

Ingredients You'll Need:

Chocolate cake baked in a 4" x 8" (10cm x 20cm) loaf pan, uniced

⅓ quantity chocolate buttercream icing (recipe on page 31)

4 ounces (113g) each milk chocolate and white chocolate candy melt

12 ounces (340g) dark chocolate candy melt

1 quantity sugar syrup (recipe on page 30)

Powdered sugar and cocoa powder (for dusting)

Supplies You'll Need:

Leaf cookie cutters

Cardboard

Cutting board

Parchment paper

Spatula

Serrated knife

Turntable

Serving platter

2. Slice and Prepare Cake

Place the uniced cake on a cutting board and cut off
the top with a serrated knife to level it. Set the top
aside for later use. Cut the remaining cake halfway
down from the top and separate. Brush each piece
with sugar syrup and spread a layer of chocolate
buttercream icing onto the tops of each piece.
Stack one layer on top of the other.

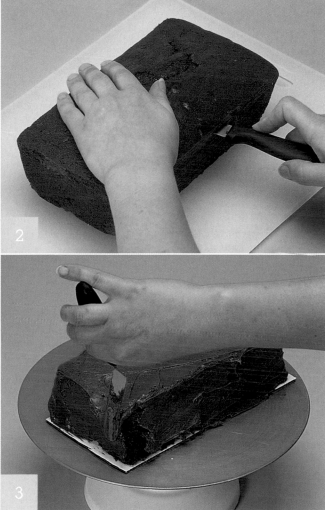

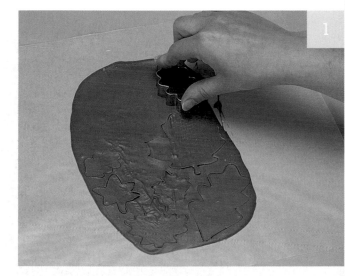

1. Make Chocolate Leaves

Pour melted milk chocolate candy melt over a
sheet of parchment paper and spread with a spatula
into a layer about ¹⁄₁₆" (0.2cm) thick. When it loses
its sheen and does not stick to your finger, press
leaf cookie cutters into the chocolate. Once it is
completely hardened, gently work away the edges
and lift the chocolate leaves with the spatula. Repeat
with all of the white chocolate candy melt and ¹⁄₃ of
the dark chocolate candy melt (the rest will be used
in step 6). The leaves will last several weeks in an
airtight container.

3. Crumb-coat Cake

Transfer the cake to a piece of cardboard cut to the
size of the cake and place it on the turntable.
Crumb-coat the cake in a thin layer of chocolate
buttercream icing (see page 20).

TIDBIT

Cut the corners of your paper to make it easier to tuck and fold.

4. Add Peaks to Cake

Cut the cake top from step 2 into several uneven pieces. Place them on top of the cake randomly to form peaks.

5. Cover Peaks with Icing

Cover the peaks with chocolate buttercream icing using a spatula.

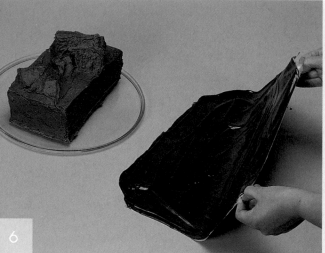

6. Cover Cake with Chocolate

Transfer the cake to a serving platter. Spread melted dark chocolate candy melt over an entire sheet of parchment paper, all the way to the edge. For a standard 4" x 8" (10cm x 20cm) loaf pan, use a sheet of parchment paper about 12" x 15" (30cm x 38cm). Before the chocolate hardens, lift the edges of the paper and flip it, chocolate-side down, onto the cake. Caution: This could get messy!

tasty
TIDBIT
Chocolate has a tendency to discolor when it is heated and cooled. Powdered sugar is a great way to camouflage this.

8. Remove Paper

Once the chocolate has hardened, peel off the parchment paper carefully.

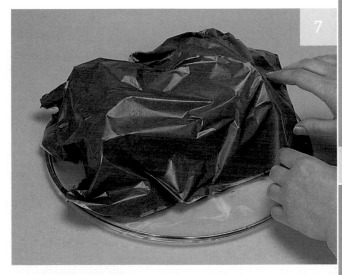

7. Fold and Tuck

Arrange the parchment paper, adding folds and tucking in edges. Allow the chocolate to harden. Make sure your creases aren't too deep or the paper will be trapped between the folds and will be difficult to remove.

9. Add Chocolate Leaves

Position the chocolate leaves from step 1 around the cake on the serving platter. Use melted chocolate to help them stick. Dust the cake with powdered sugar and cocoa powder.

variations

In this variation, I made stars out of white chocolate candy melt and painted them with edible gold powder. Edible powder is available in nearly every color at specialty cake decorating stores.

top 5 rules of working
WITH CHOCOLATE

Chocolate tastes great, but it can be a little difficult to work with. Follow these rules to ensure that your chocolate creations taste great and look beautiful.

1. Store your chocolate in a cool, dry place. The ideal storage temperature is 55°F to 75°F (13°C to 24°C) with 40% to 60% humidity. A normal air conditioned room will suffice.

2. Chocolate can be frozen for up to six months when properly stored in an airtight container. To avoid condensation when thawing, allow chocolate to thaw inside the container until it reaches room temperature.

3. Store chocolate away from direct sunlight and heat. The light will cause the color to fade, and the heat may cause melting.

4. Chocolate absorbs flavors and odors very easily. Store it away from chemicals, cleaning solvents, perfumes and air fresheners.

5. Chocolate and moisture do not mix. The moisture produces a white haze, called "bloom," on the surface of the chocolate. Bloom does not alter the taste, but it does mar the appearance.

fancy in
fondant

Fondant, also called sugar paste, can be rolled out and placed over crumb-coated cakes, sculpted into various shapes, or poured in liquid form. The cakes in this chapter are covered in rolled fondant, which is rolled out like dough and placed over a crumb-coated cake. It has the smooth appearance of porcelain and the malleable consistency of soft clay.

Fondant can be made from scratch or purchased in craft and baking supply stores. Although they work equally as well for decorating, I think homemade fondant looks and tastes much better because you can add creative colors and flavorings.

Fondant is best used on denser cakes, as light and spongy cakes may not hold up to the weight. It is important to remember that fondant will sweat after coming out of the refrigerator on a humid day. For this reason, it is best used in cooler temperatures or on cakes that will stay at room temperature (like fruitcake).

Before applying the fondant, you must level and crumb-coat your cake, since bumps will show through the fondant. Beware of putting white fondant on a cake crumb-coated in chocolate icing. The dark color will show through the translucent white fondant. White buttercream icing works best for this.

In order for the fondant to stick, you must crumb-coat the cake shortly before applying the fondant. Otherwise, the icing will form a dry layer after it has been exposed to the air.

Covering a Cake with Fondant

Covering a cake with fondant will give it a smooth, flawless finish. Be sure to start with a freshly crumb-coated cake so that the fondant sticks.

1. Prepare Fondant

Prepare the fondant (recipe on page 32) and refrigerate overnight. Remove the fondant from the refrigerator and allow it to sit, covered and at room temperature, for a few hours. Spread powdered sugar on your work surface and knead the fondant until it forms a smooth ball.

2. Shape Fondant

Shape the fondant ball into a disc. Add more powdered sugar if needed, but remember that too much will dry out the fondant.

3. Roll Out Fondant

Sprinkle powdered sugar on your work surface and rolling pin to keep the fondant from sticking. Roll out the fondant to slightly larger than your cake top.

4. Cover Cake

Transfer a freshly crumb-coated cake to a turntable and gently place the fondant over the cake.

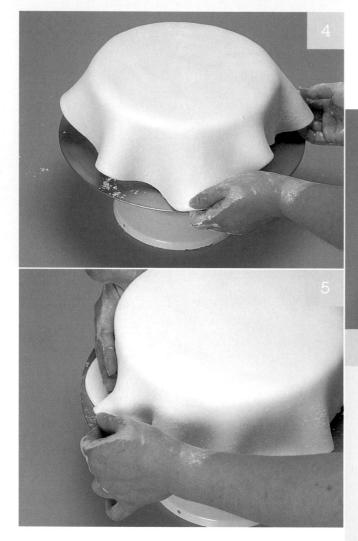

tasty
TIDBIT To remove air bubbles under the fondant, poke them with a knife and smooth with your finger.

6. Trim Excess

Trim the excess fondant from the bottom of the cake with a straight edge knife.

5. Stretch Sides

Stretch the fondant over the sides of the cake. Smooth the top and sides by moving your hands in a firm, circular motion. Slowly work down the sides, stretching the fondant gently and smoothing it with a back and forth motion.

he loves
me

This cake was my friend Katherine's idea, and I ended up making it for her wedding reception. It is the perfect sweet surprise for a bridal shower, anniversary or special Valentine! The unpretentious daisies make it fresh and lighthearted, while the fondant creates a smooth, elegant finish. To achieve the light green color, dip a toothpick in green food coloring and add to the fondant during the kneading process.

Ingredients You'll Need:

8" (20cm) round cake covered in light green fondant (see pages 100 and 101)

⅛ quantity classic buttercream icing (recipe on page 30)

Supplies You'll Need:

3 to 4 fresh daisy branches (15 to 20 flowers)

White satin floral ribbon

Cloth pastry bag

Tip: #4

Toothpick

Scissors

Turntable

Serving platter

tasty
TIDBIT You may want to practice writing on parchment paper or cardboard before trying it on your cake.

2. Pipe "He Loves Me"

Fill a pastry bag with white buttercream icing and insert tip #4. Pipe the words "He Loves Me" on the cake, using the score marks as your guide.

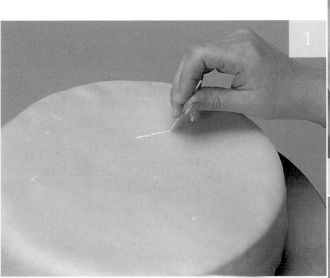

1. Cover Cake and Score Lines

Tint one quantity of fondant light green and place it over a crumb-coated cake. Place the fondant-covered cake on a turntable. Use a toothpick to score three lines across the top right side of the cake. They will help you keep your letters in line when you are piping.

3. Prepare Daisies

Cut three or four fresh daisy stems and tie them together in a cluster with white satin ribbon. Tie the ribbon into a bow and cut the edges at an angle.

4. Arrange Daisies on Cake

Place the daisy cluster on top of the cake to the left of the words. Pick all but one petal off of another daisy and sprinkle the petals over the cake. Secure the daisy center onto the cake with a dab of icing.

5. Add More Daisies

As a finishing touch, add daisy flower heads around the sides of the cake and secure with icing. Transfer the cake to a serving platter and refrigerate until ready to serve.

say it with ICING

The style of writing that you pipe should reflect the message you wish to convey and match the style of the cake. For instance, a message written in fancy script would complement an anniversary or Valentine's Day cake, and a message written in big block letters and bold colors would go great on a little boy's birthday cake. Here are a few writing styles that will give you ideas.

Congratulations!

HAPPY BIRTHDAY!

I Love You

Bon Voyage!

Dear Guests,

Please help yourselves

to cake and coffee.

violets and
vines

This cake uses royal icing flowers made on floral wires, which are bundled together in small bouquets of violets. The fondant painting technique uses food coloring to create a stunning effect. I recommend practicing on an extra piece of fondant or cardboard before going for the cake. This will give you a feel for the food coloring's consistency, and you will also be able to mix the right color green to match the violets' leaves.

*Since more than one color and type
of icing are needed for this project,
I recommend using several pastry bags.

Ingredients You'll Need:

8" (20cm) round cake covered
in white fondant (see pages 100
and 101)

2 quantities royal icing divided
into ½ green; ⅜ purple; ⅛ yellow
(recipe on page 32)

Supplies You'll Need:

Floral nail

24- or 26-gauge floral wire

Parchment paper cut into small
squares

Floral tape

Craft foam

Cloth pastry bags*

Tips: #2, 102 and 103

Food coloring paste: green

Paintbrush

Small plate

Toothpick

Water

Rolling pin

Straight edge knife/pizza cutter

Needle-nose pliers

Turntable

Serving platter

2. Pipe Bottom Petal

Using the same icing and tip as in step 1, pipe a
large bottom petal by holding the wide end of the tip
down on the nail and turning it to make a half circle.

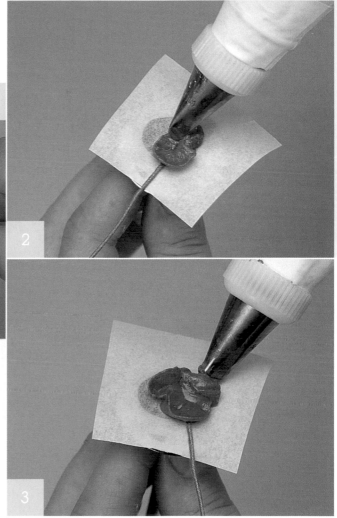

1. Add Floral Wire

Fill a pastry bag with purple royal icing and insert tip
#102. Secure a square of parchment paper to a
flower nail with a tiny bit of icing. Add a dot of icing to
the paper and place a piece of floral wire measuring
2½" to 3½" (6cm to 9cm) in the center of the dot.

3. Pipe Side Petals

Next, make two small, round side petals by holding
the wide end of the tip toward the middle of the
flower. Keep the nail stationary and make a narrow,
round shape.

4. Pipe Top Petals

To make the top two petals, point the tip upward and move the bag from the center, in a loop, and back down to the center. Remove the parchment paper from the flower nail and place it on a cookie sheet. Repeat steps 1 to 4 for the desired number of violets (I made about 20). Set them aside to harden.

tasty TIDBIT I always make a few extra violets and leaves to have on hand just in case one breaks.

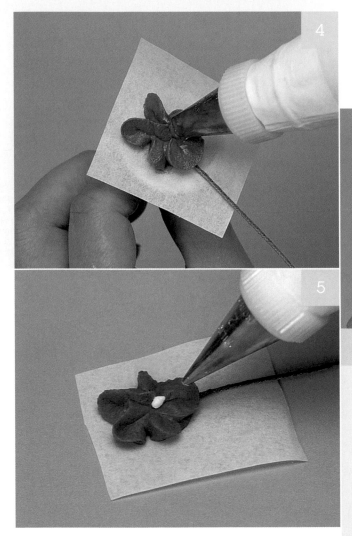

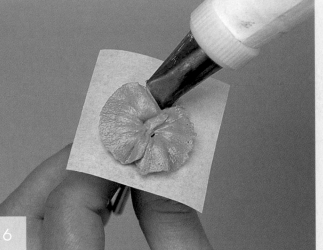

6. Pipe Leaves

Fill a pastry bag with green royal icing and insert tip #103. Add a dollop of icing and a piece of floral wire measuring 2½" to 3½" (6cm to 9cm) to the prepared flower nail. Start at one side of the wire and end at the other, keeping the pastry bag stationary and turning the nail all the way around to form a leaf. Remove the parchment paper from the flower nail and place it on a cookie sheet. Repeat to make several more leaves and set aside to harden.

5. Pipe Stamens

Fill a pastry bag with yellow royal icing and insert tip #2. Once the violets have hardened, pipe a yellow stamen in the center of each violet.

8. Wrap Clusters Together

Use floral tape to wrap two royal icing violets together at the stems. Add leaves and more violets, wrapping each time with floral tape. I used five clusters of three violets and three leaves for the sides of the cake and one larger bouquet of five to seven violets and five to seven leaves for the top. Stick the violet clusters in craft foam and store until needed.

tasty TIDBIT Since regular floral tape is too wide for these tiny clusters, I recommend cutting it in half down the middle.

7. Pipe Details

Onco the violets have hardened, dip a small paintbrush in purple food coloring and paint three to tive lines on the bottom petal of each violet.

9. Prepare Your Paint

On a small plate, use a toothpick to mix white and green food coloring to match the color of the violet leaves.

10. Paint Vines, Leaves and Tendrils

Place the fondant-covered cake on the turntable and trim away the excess. Set aside for later use. Dip a very small paintbrush in the light green food coloring paste and paint vines, leaves and tendrils on the top and sides of the cake.

tasty
TIDBIT A pizza cutter works great for cutting fondant!

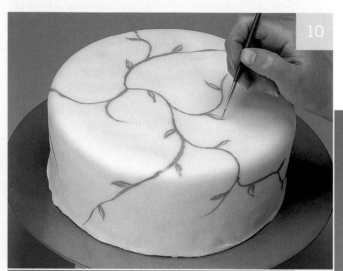

12. Add Violet Clusters

Transfer the cake to a serving platter. Add all but one of the royal icing violet clusters around the base of the cake, bending the floral wires and tucking them under the cake. Use needle-nose pliers to stick a final violet cluster on the top of the cake.

11. Make Fondant Ribbon

To make a ribbon around the cake, retrieve the extra fondant from step 10 and tint it light green. Roll it into a thin strip measuring the diameter of the cake. Trim the edges of the fondant with a pizza cutter or straight edge knife. Adhere the fondant ribbon around the bottom edge of the cake with water, rotating the turntable as necessary.

christmas
package

You'll surely impress all your friends with this stunning holiday cake. It can easily be adapted to be a birthday present as well. Mix and match your favorite stamps and colors to customize the cake. The possibilities are endless!

Ingredients You'll Need:

8" (20cm) square cake covered in white fondant* (see pages 100 and 101)

1/8 quantity classic buttercream icing (see page 30)

Supplies You'll Need:

Cookie sheet

Polyester batting

Food coloring paste: green, yellow and red

Food coloring liquid: white

Food coloring powder: blue

Paintbrush

Four small plates

Toothpick

Christmas tree stamp

Star stamp

Rolling pin

Straight edge knife/pizza cutter

Turntable

Serving platter

*You will need to 1 1/2 quantities of fondant to cover this square cake. Double the recipe on page 32 and use the rest to make the bow and ribbons.

1. Make Bow Pieces

Cover the cake in fondant, trim away excess and set the cake aside. Roll out a thin piece the excess fondant and use a pizza cutter or straight edge knife to cut out two loop pieces and two streamer pieces, each measuring 1½" x 5" (4cm x 13cm). Fold each loop in half, stick the ends together and pinch with your fingers to secure. Fill with polyester batting. Next, cut out a center piece measuring 1½" x 2" (4cm x 5cm). Pinch the ends and tuck them under to make a ring. Fill the piece with polyester batting.

2. Finish Bow Pieces

Pinch one end of each streamer and cut a "V" shape at the other end. Stuff with polyester batting to hold the shape. Place all the bow pieces on a cookie sheet and set aside to harden for at least 24 hours.

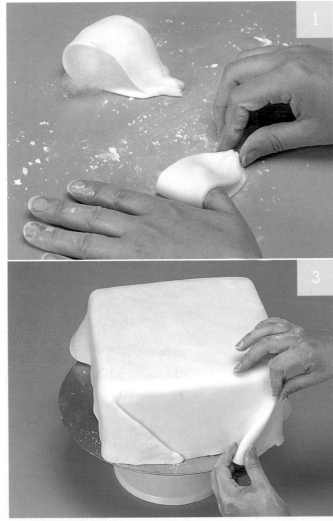

3. Form Fondant Package

Place the fondant-covered cake on the turntable and smooth the fondant with your hands to work out any air pockets. Gather the excess fondant from the sides and tuck inward like the folds of a package as shown. Press firmly against the cake to adhere. Use a straight edge knife to trim the excess.

4. Stamp Decorations

Pour small amounts of green, yellow and red food coloring paste onto small plates and add a drop of white food coloring liquid to the green. Dip a Christmas tree stamp into the green food coloring and stamp randomly onto the fondant. Stamp yellow stars randomly in between the trees and use a paintbrush to touch up any light spots. Dot the trees with ornaments using a toothpick and red food coloring.

5. Paint Cake

Pour a small amount of blue food coloring powder onto a plate. Dip the paintbrush into the powder paint in all the white spaces on the fondant. Add more powder to the plate as needed.

tasty

TIDBIT As an alternative to food coloring pow der, dry nontoxic pastels can be used. Scrape the end of the pastel with a craft knife to make a fine powder.

6. Make Ribbons

Using the remaining fondant from step 1, roll out two long strips to make the ribbons on the package. The width should measure 1½" (4cm). The length should be as long as the top and two sides of the cake. For example, this cake measures 8" (20cm) in diameter and stands 4½" (11cm) tall. Therefore, each ribbon should measure approximately 17" (43cm). Adhere the ribbons horizontally and vertically across the cake with buttercream icing to secure. Trim the edges with a straight edge knife.

7. Add Bow

Remove the polyester batting from the bow in steps 1 and 2 and assemble it on top of the cake. Adhere the bow and streamers with buttercream icing. Transfer to a serving platter.

heart
mini-cakes

The possibilities for these heart mini-cakes are endless. You can decorate them any way your heart desires. It's fun to make each one slightly different and allow your guests to eat their personal favorite! This project uses one of my favorite techniques – brushing food coloring onto fondant with a medium paintbrush or pastry brush. Your imagination and creative talents will have free reign to design fun and unique variations.

Ingredients You'll Need:

Sheet cake baked on a 9" x 13" (23cm x 33cm) cookie sheet, uniced

Fondant in various shades of pink* (recipe on page 32)

Classic buttercream icing* (recipe on page 30)

Pasteurized egg whites

Water

Supplies You'll Need:

Heart-shaped cookie cutters in various sizes

⅛" (0.3cm) wide floral ribbon (optional)

24- or 26-gauge floral wire

Cutting board or hard surface

Rolling pin

Food coloring paste: red

Medium paintbrush or pastry brush

*Fondant and buttercream icing quantities
will depend on the amount of mini-cakes and
fondant decorations made, as well as the size
of the cookie cutters.

1. Make Fondant Heart Decorations

Roll out thin sheets of fondant in various shades of pink and use cookie cutters to cut out hearts of all different sizes. Coat 3" (8cm) pieces of floral wire with pasteurized egg whites and insert them into the fondant hearts. Transfer to parchment paper and allow to dry for at least 24 hours.

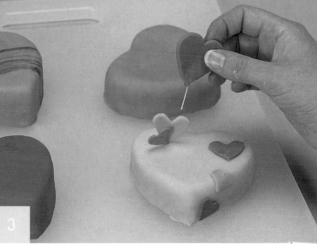

3. Add Fondant Hearts

When the decorations from step 1 are dry, trim the floral wires as necessary and stick them into the heart mini-cakes. Use excess fondant to cut out additional hearts and adhere them to the sides of the cakes with water. Add ⅛" (0.3cm) wide floral ribbon if desired.

2. Decorate Cakes

Use the largest heart cookie cutter to cut out heart shapes from the cake. Crumb-coat the cakes with white buttercream icing (see page 20) and cover them with fondant, stretching and smoothing with your hands (see pages 100 and 101). Crease the fondant at the top of the hearts. Use different colors of fondant to add your own flair. For a streaked look, dip a medium paintbrush or pastry brush in red paste food coloring and drag it across the top of the cake.

4. Decorate Several Cakes

Decorate several heart mini-cakes at a time, mixing and matching the colors, shapes and designs to your heart's content!

tasty
TIDBIT To make different shades of pink fondant, start by adding dark pink food coloring paste with a toothpick and gradually add drops of white food coloring liquid.

mini-cakes for
EVERY OCCASION!

With mini-cakes, the shapes and decorating possibilities are endless. Why not invite your friends over for a mini-cake-making party. Each person can bring a cookie cutter and some decorations. Here are a few ideas:

Christmas Tree Mini-Cakes: Use a triangle cookie cutter to cut out the shapes from a large sheet cake. Cover with green fondant. Use buttercream icing to stick small chocolate candies to the tree and add a square of semisweet chocolate at the bottom for a trunk.

Easter Egg Mini-Cakes: Use an oval cookie cutter to cut out Easter egg shapes from a large sheet cake. Tint several portions of fondant in different pastel colors. Cover the eggs with fondant and add pastel polka dots, stripes and zigzags.

Birthday Present Mini-Cakes: Cut squares and rectangles from a large sheet cake. Tint several portions of fondant in different bright colors. Cover the cakes with the fondant and add fondant ribbon and decorations in contrasting colors.

Spooky Halloween Mini-Cakes: Use alphabet cookie cutters to cut out the letters B-O-O. Separate fondant into three sections and color them orange, black and white. Cover each letter with a different color fondant, trimming around the holes and smoothing with your fingers. Transfer to a serving dish and decorate with fake cobwebs and plastic spiders.

cool citrus
dream cake

This cake uses delicate royal icing piping on fondant and a ribbon weaving technique. For a tangy taste of citrus, add orange zest to the cake batter, sugar syrup and filling. Or, try adding a thin layer of lemon curd between each layer as you fill your cake.

Ingredients You'll Need:

8" (20cm) round cake covered in white fondant (see pages 100 and 101)

½ quantity white royal icing (recipe on page 32)

Orange slices

Supplies You'll Need:

15⁄16" (3cm) and 9⁄16" (1cm) orange satin floral ribbon

Cloth pastry bag

Tip: #1

Straight edge knife

Scissors

Turntable

Serving platter

1. Pipe Dot Clusters

Place the fondant-covered cake on the turntable. Fill a pastry bag with white royal icing and insert tip #1. Add three-dot clusters randomly over the entire cake.

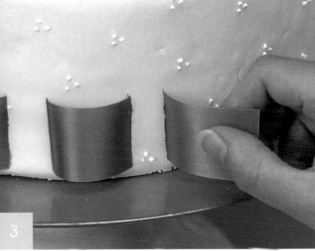

3. Weave Ribbon into Slits

Work your way around the cake, weaving pieces of ribbon into each slit.

2. Cut Slits in Fondant

Cut out several pieces of the thicker orange floral ribbon about 1" (2.5cm) long. Use a straight edge knife to cut slits around the bottom perimeter of the cake, piercing the fondant just enough to "weave" the ribbons into the slits.

4. Arrange Orange Slices

Cut and twist thin orange slices and arrange them in a decorative star pattern on top of the cake.

5. Add Ribbon to Top of Cake

Cut slits in the top of the cake between the orange slices. Cut out five pieces of the thinner ribbon to about 1/2" (1.3cm) long and weave the ribbons into the slits. Transfer to a serving platter and refrigerate until ready to serve.

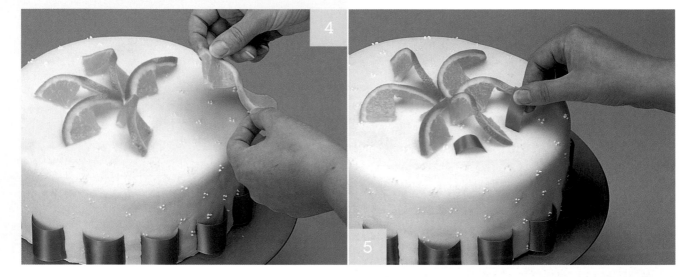

variation

Change this cake slightly by using limes, dot clusters of green royal icing and two colors of green ribbon.

Resources

All of the ingredients and supplies in this book can be found at your local grocery or craft store. For more specialized tools or a better selection, I have provided a list of resources. Most of these companies offer catalogs and have web sites for easy ordering. Also, be sure to consult your local yellow pages for cake decorating stores in your area.

Suppliers

Beryl's Cake Decorating and
Pastry Supplies

P.O. Box 1584
North Springfield, VA 22151-0584
United States
Phone: 1-800-488-2749
Fax: 703-750-3779
Web site: www.beryls.com
Email: beryls@beryls.com

The Bonbonerie

2030 Madison Rd.
Cincinnati, OH 45208
Phone: (513) 321-3399
Fax: (513) 979-5332
Web site: www.thebonbon.com

The Chef's Catalog

Customer Relations
P.O. Box 650589
Dallas, TX 75265-0589
Phone: 1-800-884-CHEF
Web site: www.chefscatalog.com

Creative Cutters

561 Edward Ave.
Units 1 and 2
Richmond Hill, Ontario
Canada L4C-9W6
Phone: 1-888 805-3444
Web site:
www.creativecutters.com
Email: products@creativecutters.com

Hobby Lobby

7707 SW 44th St.
Oklahoma City, OK 73179
Web site: www.hobbylobby.com

Michael's

8000 Bent Branch Dr.
Irving, TX 75063
Phone: 1-800-MICHAELS (1-800-642-4235)
Web site: www.michaels.com

New York Cake Supplies

56 West 22nd St.
New York, NY 10010
Phone: (800) 942-2539
Fax: (212) 675-7099
Web site: www.nycake.com

Wilton Industries, Inc.

2240 West 75th Street
Woodridge, IL 60517
Phone: 1-800-794-5866
Fax: 1-888-824-9520
Web site: www.wilton.com
Email: info@wilton.com

Books and Publications

These books and magazines offer a multitude of recipes and project ideas as well as resources.

American Cake Decorating magazine

Every issue features quick and easy decorating ideas, tips and techniques for mastering the basics and step-by-step projects for every skill level.

The Cake Bible

By Rose-Levy Beranbaum
Experienced baker and author Beranbaum explains the science of baking, including ingredients, tools and materials, recipes, tips and techniques.

Cakes

By Maida Heatter
Kitchen pro Heatter shares her recipes, tips and tricks for baking easy to fancy cakes, from chocolate cake to cheesecake to cupcakes and more.

Cakes by Design

By Scott Clark Woolley and Michael G. Farace
The masters of making sugar paste flowers give step by step instructions for how to create calla lilies, tulips and other flowers out of sugar.

Storybook Cakes

By Lindy Smith
This collection of lively, fun cake designs is based on favorite stories and fairy tales that will delight both children and adults.

Index

The best craft projects come from North Light Books!

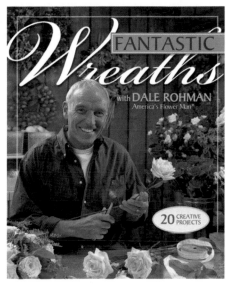

Fabulous Cake Decorating

Whether you're celebrating a birthday, wedding, shower or any occasion, this fun guide provides bakers and do-it-yourselfers with dazzling ideas and techniques for decorating a variety of cakes. Fully illustrated steps and detailed captions guide you in making more than 25 inspirational cakes showcasing a range of styles and effects with readily available ingredients.

ISBN 1-55870-549-X, paperback, 128 pages, #70479-K

Silk Florals for the Holidays

Make your holidays brighter and more special by creating your very own floral decor! Cele Kahle shows you how to create a variety of gorgeous arrangements, swags, topiaries, wreaths and even bows. There are 19 creative projects in all, using silk foliage, berries, fruit and ribbon. Each one comes with materials lists, step-by-step guidelines and beautiful full-color photos.

ISBN 1-58180-259-5, paperback, 128 pages, #32124-K

Fantastic Wreaths with Dale Rohman

Nothing makes a home more inviting than an elegant wreath or swag on the front door. In this inspiring book, floral designer Dale Rohman shows you how to make your own door decor with his helpful hints and mini-demos. You'll find 20 amazing step-by-step projects in all, utilizing a huge variety of intriguing materials including fresh roses, apples, limes, banana peppers, sea shells, tropical flowers and more!

ISBN 1-58180-289-7, paperback, 128 pages, #32165-K

These and other fine North Light titles are available from your local art & craft retailer, bookstore, online supplier or by calling 1-800-448-0915.